to ?... . Infinity

dear frie
the first to host a HOS workshop

With love and gratitude

Pierre   Geneviève

Vernou 20 juin 2016

Becoming Who You Are
with the
Intelligence of Self

Understanding one's psychological type
and developing fully with Voice Dialogue

Pierre Cauvin
Geneviève Cailloux

BALBOA
PRESS
A DIVISION OF HAY HOUSE

Copyright © 2016 Pierre Cauvin-Geneviève Cailloux.

All rights reserved. No part of this book may be used or reproduced by any means, graphic, electronic, or mechanical, including photocopying, recording, taping or by any information storage retrieval system without the written permission of the author except in the case of brief quotations embodied in critical articles and reviews.

Balboa Press books may be ordered through booksellers or by contacting:

Balboa Press
A Division of Hay House
1663 Liberty Drive
Bloomington, IN 47403
www.balboapress.com
1 (877) 407-4847

Because of the dynamic nature of the Internet, any web addresses or links contained in this book may have changed since publication and may no longer be valid. The views expressed in this work are solely those of the author and do not necessarily reflect the views of the publisher, and the publisher hereby disclaims any responsibility for them.

The author of this book does not dispense medical advice or prescribe the use of any technique as a form of treatment for physical, emotional, or medical problems without the advice of a physician, either directly or indirectly. The intent of the author is only to offer information of a general nature to help you in your quest for emotional and spiritual well-being. In the event you use any of the information in this book for yourself, which is your constitutional right, the author and the publisher assume no responsibility for your actions.

Any people depicted in stock imagery provided by Thinkstock are models, and such images are being used for illustrative purposes only.
Certain stock imagery © Thinkstock.

Print information available on the last page.

ISBN: 978-1-5043-4610-8 (sc)
ISBN: 978-1-5043-4611-5 (e)

Library of Congress Control Number: 2015921238

Balboa Press rev. date: 3/22/2016

For Hal and Sidra Stone
With our deepest gratitude

Endorsement
By Dr Roger Pearman

Mary McCaulley Lifetime Achievement Award
Past President of the Association
for Psychological Type international

Pierre Cauvin and Genevieve Cailloux have masterfully integrated their years of experience and deep subject matter expertise in the writing of **Becoming who you are with the Intelligence of Self**. Written in an accessible style, complete with stories and examples, you cannot help but be pulled into the journey of the psyche in compelling and inspiring ways. They have refreshed and deepened Carl Jung's exploration of the eight functions (e.g. Extraverted Thinking, Introverted Sensing, etc.) by linking these elements of the psyche to the matters of adapting to everyday challenges. The linkage of the power of naming, unhooking, integrating, and rebalancing with the opposite for each of the dominant mental functions adds greatly to the understanding of the power of psychological type to enrich our lives. Through the practical example of people's lives, Cauvin and Cailloux have provided illustrations for how the positive and negative energies generate patterns of our types can entrap or enrich our relationships. Learning from others' trials is critical if you want to build on understanding what to do in future circumstances. With clarity and compassion, they have provided techniques that give us practical guidance for using our self intelligence in ways that maximize our gifts leading to fulfillment and empower our relationships for resulting in well-being.

Foreword
By Hal Stone PhD & Sidra Stone PhD
Founders of the Voice Dialogue

Pierre Cauvin and Geneviève Cailloux describe their book, "Becoming Who You Are with The Intelligence of Self", as "the culmination of everything [they] have learned and transmitted throughout [their] personal and professional lives, up to this moment". It is clear from the wealth of material that this book contains, that they have learned and transmitted a great deal. This book is a rich feast of information, ideas, and experiences combined with a great deal of practical advice and wisdom based on their long years of experience in coaching and teaching.

This is an excellent time - in the fullness and maturity of their professional lives - for them to share the bounties they have harvested. And we nod in appreciation as we read their caveat: "up to this moment". Because they well know that their journey is not over; that there will be more explorations and discoveries; and that there will be more to come. This is why their work is so exciting. Their work is not encased in cement. Their own Intelligence of Self doesn't allow them to become identified to wherever they are in their current thinking and writing. So it is that they continue to expand into ever-widening fields of exploration.

Cauvin and Cailloux are scholars and adventurers who have spent a lifetime of study and teaching. The Intelligence of Self is rich with their knowledge of the psyche and how it operates. It is a real work of scholarship. Weaving together a rich and complex fabric that includes both the Jungian Psychological Types (widely used in the business community) and the more recent Voice Dialogue and the Psychology of Selves (giving direct access to the selves represented by these types), they have created a system that appeals to the mind, gives access to the emotions, and certainly warms the heart.

This meticulous presentation of their work is a combination of erudition and an ability to present complex material with clarity and simplicity. It is enlivened and enriched by a broad range of illustrative case studies that are based on Cailloux' and Cauvin's extensive direct experience as coaches, facilitators, and teachers. The case material they use to illustrate their work with coaching in corporate environments was of particular interest to us because we have not seen this kind of material elsewhere. We found it quite amazing to see their work helping to shift the consciousness of a major corporate entity.

The Intelligence of Self gives the reader access to a new world of experience. It is a simple idea once we have the experience of separating from a part of our own "Auto-pilot" system. The Auto-pilot is another way of describing what we call the "operating ego". Calling these selves the "Auto-pilot" creates a powerful image in our minds of the automatic regulation that characterizes these selves that run our lives until we have the opportunity to separate from them. Once we are able to separate from this Auto-pilot, there is the possibility of experiencing and embracing new ways of looking at the world, new ways of being in our lives, new energies, new kinds of creativity, new solutions to old problems, and untold unexpected discoveries as our disowned energy systems, or selves, are given the chance to emerge.

How Cauvin and Cailloux tie all of this work with selves to the work with Psychological Types is a fascinating process. First they developed and clarified their own work with the Types. Next, they worked with the selves and built a system of solid bridges to their work with Voice Dialogue, the Psychology of Selves and the Aware Ego. Then, because of their coaching background, they developed strong connections to the business world and so were able to build yet another bridge connecting these two to the world of coaching in business. The result is a lovely set of interconnecting methodologies, ideologies, and skill sets to make it all work – and it most certainly does work!

This brings us to our professional and personal relationship with Geneviève and Pierre. They had been immersed in the work with Pyschological Types training for many years, first with the MBTI, then with their own questionnaire, the CCTI. It was their own search for new ways of working and thinking and coaching as well as their constant search for self knowledge that eventually led them into the methodology of Voice Dialogue and then into the whole theoretical structure of the Psychology of Selves and the Aware Ego. From all of this, they have created The Intelligence of Self: their unique and major contribution as consciousness teachers to the field of coaching.

For many years their work was driven by their own thirst for a deeper consciousness in relationship to their own individual processes and to the process of the relationship, itself. They have always worked intensively on their personal and relational process. They remain seekers forever and this is what makes their work so rich and gives it such depth. It is grounded in their own search for consciousness and for a conscious relationship.

We have had the privilege of sharing with Pierre and Genevieve many moments of intimacy as we have travelled alongside them on their personal journey. There is one additional comment that we would like to make; one that we feel sums up their lives and their latest book. "**Pierre and Geneviève *are* what they teach!**" That is how we can best describe who they are, what they stand for, and what this book is about. And, for us, this is the highest compliment that can be given to any teacher, or to any couple, who teach the work of consciousness.

Albion, California
September 4, 2015

Table of Contents

Introduction: Opening the Doors of the Psyche xvii

PART I
THE INTELLIGENCE OF SELF: FROM THE AUTO-PILOT TO THE AWARE EGO; THE OPERATING PRINCIPLES OF THE PSYCHE 1

1. BETWEEN LIGHT AND SHADOW; THE 8 PSYCHIC FUNCTIONS 5
    The 8 Functions 5
    Order of Integration of the Functions 16
2. SPONTANEOUS EVOLUTION OF THE PSYCHE: THE AUTO-PILOT (OR OPERATING EGO) 27
    Adaptation Strategies 27
    The Auto-Pilot (The Operating Ego) 32
    The Three Laws Of Natural Evolution 38
    A Turf War 42
3. SELF-DEVELOPMENT WITH INTELLIGENCE: THE AWARE EGO 48
    The Three Laws Of Conscious Evolution 48
    The Aware Ego 55
4. THE INTELLIGENCE OF SELF AND OF THE OTHER 61
    Bonding Patterns 61
    Projections And Judgments 66

PART II
PUTTING THE INTELLIGENCE OF SELF INTO PRACTICE .. 75

5. SOME TYPICAL SITUATIONS 77
    Childhood 77
    Intimate Relationships (Couples) 83
    The Aging Process 91
    Career And Professional Mobility 94

	Management Positions...101
	The Aware Ego And Politics 108
6.	INTELLIGENCE OF SELF, INTELLIGENCE OF THE COACH..111
	The Coach's Posture: Who Is Coaching? 112
	The Various Stages Of Coaching..121
	The Coaching Relationship 129
7.	FIVE TECHNIQUES TO HELP YOU ALONG THE PATH 141
	Voice Dialogue 141
	Personality Types 146
	Active Imagination 147
	Taking Back Projections 155
	By The Light Of Our Dreams 159
8.	SELF-COACHING THROUGH THE INSIGHTS OF INTELLIGENCE OF SELF 167
	Practical Tips.. 168
	Identify Your Operating System..170
	Disidentifying The Auto-Pilot 174
	Integrating The Shadow 176
9.	INTELLIGENCE OF SELF IN ACTION.................................... 180
	Introduction 180
	Reframing A Difficulty In One Session 181
	Coaching With Intelligence Of Self...................................... 184
	Intelligence Of Self And Mediation 189
	Coaching For Couples Or Associates 194
	Coaching Business Associates 198
	Using Intelligence Of Self To Help Student Groups 205
	Intelligence Of Self And Projections 208

Conclusion 215
Glossary 219
Index Of Literary References.. 225
Bibliography... 233
Acknowledgements... 237
Information, Interventions, Training... 239
Index Of Illustrations... 243
Index Of Tables... 245

Introductory Note
By Kim Wall

So many of us spend our lives looking outward to find happiness, running from conflict, and sitting in judgment of others. What if we could recognize our "triggers", get clarity on the imbalances within our psyche, understand how our imbalances affect us and our relationships, and create a roadmap towards changing our own conscious awareness? What if we could literally re-create ourselves one step at a time, from the inside out?

I was originally introduced to the Cailloux-Cauvin Type Indicator (CCTI) and The Intelligence of Self (TIOS), which was in its formative stages, at a Voice Dialogue Convergence in Gwatt, Switzerland, in the fall of 2004.

I had been using Voice Dialogue with my clients for many years, and I had recently heard how others in the Voice Dialogue community were using it in conjunction with Pierre and Genevieve's CCTI and TIOS. The combination of these two approaches provide both a solid framework for discovering one's type and a powerful technique for creating a roadmap to assist clients in understanding and developing their psyche.

I felt that this method was exactly what I had been looking for and enrolled in an intensive CCTI/TIOS training course with Pierre and Geneviève in Austin, Texas in 2014. It was powerful for me to discover my type, to map it out psychologically, and to see where my own imbalances were. Learning that I could actually SEE the imbalances and DO something to bring balance to the under developed aspects of my personality was so exciting. I knew I would need to be able to reference this information, so I made an inquiry about purchasing their book and to my disappointment, discovered it was only available in French. Based on my experience, I knew that this book would be of great benefit to other English-speaking coaches, therapists, and teachers worldwide, so I asked Pierre and Geneviève if they would be open to creating an English version. While they considered the possibilities, I located a translator... and the rest is history!

The roadmap to a place of inner peace, happiness, and healthier relationships is, in fact, within each of us...and this book can help you get there!

Introduction

OPENING THE DOORS OF THE PSYCHE

THE INTELLIGENCE OF SELF (TIOS)[1] represents the culmination of everything we have learned and transmitted throughout our personal and professional lives, up to this moment. This book has, for that reason, several sources:

- ✓ Those who inspired us either through their own work, particularly CG Jung, or through the learning we experienced in their presence. They are many, and all contributed to enriching our own work. In the course of the last 15 years, the influence of Hal and Sidra Stone[2] has been crucial; this book owes much to them.
- ✓ Those with whom we have shared our experiences as well, whether through training courses, or individual or team coaching sessions: for this, we thank all our clients and our team of coaches. Because it is through teaching and practice that our approach was developed and refined. Theory informs practice, and practice sustains theory.

Conception and comparison to reality are integral to fully understanding that reality.

This is why it is a matter of "intelligence". According to the New American Oxford Dictionary, "Intelligence is the propensity to acquire and apply knowledge and skills". It is the propensity to put to best use the whole range of one's faculties – physical, cognitive, emotive, and psychic – in order to become capable of autonomous interaction in one's environment. For

---

[1] Intelligence of Self is a registered trademark of Osiris Conseil
[2] Hal Stone and Sidra Stone are therapists from California who, since the 1970s, have elaborated a developmental process, Voice Dialogue or Psychology of the Aware Ego. Their work has become known in France under the title of "Dialogue Intérieur" and has undergone a variety of applications. We have undertaken intensive training with them, and we continue to do so.

our purposes, "intelligence" has nothing to do with IQ measured on a test. Intelligent individuals are those who know their strengths and limitations sufficiently well enough to conduct themselves as interdependent human beings, autonomous yet interconnected with others.

To achieve this, THE INTELLIGENCE OF SELF (TIOS) will offer us the keys to our psyche, thereby enabling us to open its doors.

In the first part of this book we will present the principles, and we will explore:

- the elements constituting the psyche and the way it functions;
- the laws of evolution of the psyche – spontaneous or deliberate, "with intelligence".

We will then review some practical applications in a variety of forms:

- typical situations that most of us will encounter in the course of our lives;
- the role of coach, whose job is to assist the client to progress along the path;
- methods and tools to make use of the Intelligence of Self;
- the ways every individual can benefit from using this method;
- some examples from the experience of the TIOS practitioners.

Notes:

- *Terms are defined in the Glossary section at the end of the book .*
- *Masculine pronouns (he/him/his) have been used throughout for simplicity without any intention to exclude the feminine.*
- *The symbol † indicates that further information can be found in the Index of Literary References, particularly for the Archetypes and Celebrities listed in Tables 1.2 to 1.9,.*

PART I

THE INTELLIGENCE OF SELF: FROM THE AUTO-PILOT TO THE AWARE EGO; THE OPERATING PRINCIPLES OF THE PSYCHE

IN THE SPRING OF 2008, *La Grande Allée* of the *Jardin des Plantes* (the main promenade of the botanical gardens) in Paris was temporarily named "l'Allée du temps" (the Path of Time). The great epochs of life were laid out along the path, from the Earth's formation, some 4.5 billion years earlier, to the appearance of the first hominid, around 3 million years ago. The pathway recounted a tale of closely interrelated processes of differentiation and increasing complexity:

- cosmic gases condense and create the Earth (4.5 billion years ago)
- air and water arise from steam (4.4 billion years ago)
- photosynthesis causes separation of oxygen and carbon dioxide (2.8 billion years ago)
- sexual reproduction brings about a diversification of life forms
- (1.5 billion years ago)
- cellular life forms into organisms (1 billion years ago)
- organisms form in relation to their environment: shells and skeletons appear (540 million years ago)
- vegetation and animal life appear progressively through interactive environmental processes (440 million years ago)
- one species walks upright and distinguishes itself from the others (3 million years ago).

At each step along the way, we begin to see two complementary forces at work:

- one force leading toward separation, toward differentiation,
- the other leading toward interaction, toward association.

Each of these forces has a role and a function in evolutionary progress. If one prevails, to the detriment of the other, the evolutionary process comes to a halt:

- either due to excess separation, leading to rigidity, "sclerosis"
- or due to excess interaction, leading to fusion and assimilation of one into the other.

These two forces, which are at work throughout the evolutionary history of species (phylogenesis), appear in identical fashion in the development of the individual (ontogenesis). They are the basis of what Jung called the principle of individuation, "a process by which a being becomes an undivided psychological being – in other words, an autonomous, integrated unit, an entity unto itself"[3].

From birth, or even as early as conception, the developing human is created through processes of differentiation and ongoing interaction with its environment. This is evident in physiological development from the embryonic to the adult stage. And it is equally true in the development of the psyche: information is received by the sensory system, answers are given in response to perceived stimuli, choices must be made, decisions – intentional or otherwise – must be acted upon; psychic functions become differentiated. Long after the physical body has reached complete differentiation, psychic differentiation continues.

This psychic differentiation often occurs in a spontaneous, unconscious fashion, due to pressures related to events and the environment. But given the distinguishing feature of human beings – our capacity for reflection and distancing or detaching ourselves – we can also encourage a more lucid and deliberate process by improving our "Intelligence of Self". This brings us, therefore, to consider the following:

- The elements constituting the psyche, or the psychic functions.
- The adaptation strategies developed by the psyche in reaction to events.
- Our evolution "with intelligence", which requires awareness.
- Our interaction with other human beings.

---

[3] Translated from JUNG, Carl Gustav. *La Guérison psychologique*. Paris: Buchet Chastel, 1953

1

BETWEEN LIGHT AND SHADOW; THE 8 PSYCHIC FUNCTIONS

IN *PSYCHOLOGICAL TYPES*, CG Jung shed light on the existence of the eight functions at work in the psychic life of every individual, and how their processes differ from one individual to the next[4]. Let us consider the two elements which have the most relevance for our approach:

- the nature of the eight functions
- their order of appearance in the life of the psyche.

THE 8 FUNCTIONS

For Jung, the functions are the framework of the life of the psyche. They are processes, methods – they do not imply a specific content. To use an analogy from the field of computer technology, your computer makes use of an operating system and a variety of software to write, draw, and calculate, and these are the processes; with them, you can create specific content – for example you can write a novel or a composition, do your personal accounting, or create works of art, and these are the specific content. The eight psychological functions are the tools at our disposal to:

- gather information (Perceiving functions), and
- process and evaluate information in order to make decisions (Judging functions).

---

[4] Interested readers may wish to refer to our earlier books (see Bibliography) for a thorough description of this process

These eight functions exist in pairs of opposites. The abbreviations in parentheses are generally used to represent each function:

- Extraverted Sensing (Se) – Introverted Intuiting (Ni)
- Introverted Sensing (Si) – Extraverted Intuiting (Ne)
- Extraverted Thinking (Te) – Introverted Feeling (Fi)
- Introverted Thinking (Ti) – Extraverted Feeling (Fe).

The idea of "opposition" is fundamental, and we will encounter it again and again. It should be understood as the difference of polarity which causes energy flow, just as electrical current needs a positive pole and a negative pole. Opposition can lead to exclusion, where one element can exist only by suppressing the other. It can also be understood as tension, creating dynamism and leading to complementarity.

If one function exists alone in the psyche, without the counterbalancing effect of its opposite, there is a risk of excess, imbalance, unilateralism. Although we make use of the eight functions differently (and we will see this in the next section), we definitely need each one of them.

Table 1.1 below summarizes the principal character of each function. Tables 1.2 to 1.9 will further explore the detailed characteristics of each function under the following headings:

- Nature: the very essence of the function, the basic process
- Symbol: a visual analogy representing the function; it is often used by those who use it preferentially.
- Key word: a word or expression summing up the fundamental drive or impulse
- Archetype: from the pantheon of Greek mythology, the god who seemingly best represents the function (The symbol † indicates entries in the Index of Literary References).
- Celebrities: well-known individuals or imaginary characters related to the function (The symbol † indicates entries in the Index of Literary References).
- General characteristics

- Specific characteristics related to:
  - learning
  - problem-solving
  - leadership
  - professional life
- Potential risks: possible problem areas if the function is used excessively, without the counterbalancing effect of the opposite pole.

Table 1.1 – Summary of the 8 Functions

Function	Abbr	Propensity to...
Extraverted Sensing	Se	Immerse oneself totally in the present moment and experience the surroundings through all the senses.
Introverted Intuiting	Ni	Perceive the underlying links between diverse elements and synthesize them in a global, long-term vision.
Introverted Sensing	Si	Categorize, classify, and archive experiences and information and make use of previous learning.
Extraverted Intuiting	Ne	Produce a flow of new ideas and possibilities in any situation, at any time.
Extraverted Thinking	Te	Organize and structure the surroundings in a logical, orderly, and efficient manner.
Introverted Feeling	Fi	Create harmony around deeply felt personal values.
Introverted Thinking	Ti	Look for a rational explanation for everything through constant questioning and re-evaluation.
Extraverted Feeling	Fe	Be in harmony with others based on objective, shared values.

Table 1.2 – Extraverted Sensing (Se)

Nature	Propensity to immerse oneself totally in the present moment and experience the surroundings through all the senses
Symbol	A hand (the ability to act)
Key word	How? How to manage? How to get the job done? What's it for?
Archetype[†]	Dionysus/Bacchus – god of music, dance, wine
Celebrities[†]	Robinson Crusoe, Marie Antoinette, MacGyver, the grasshopper in Jean de la Fontaine's fable "The Ant and the Grasshopper"
General character traits	Realism, pragmatism, adaptability; moves easily from one activity to the next Unlimited energy in the areas that interest him; low energy for things seen as "duties" Dislikes rules and procedures, categories Attuned to and energized by the exterior world
Learning	Learns through practical experience and through discussion with peers Practical common sense and solutions
Problem-solving	Observant of surroundings, can sense "the lay of the land," ability to seek out necessary information Asks questions, notices changes in environment Finds practical solutions
Leadership	Leads by example and effectiveness in the field Likes hands-on involvement Resistant to hierarchical authority
Professional life	Situations which require efficiency and which are results-oriented; troubleshooting abilities Negotiation, sales; engineering, mechanics
Potential risks	Inconsistency, rejection of theoretical, lack of long term vision

Table 1.3 – Introverted Intuiting (Ni)

Nature	Propensity to perceive the underlying links between diverse elements and synthesize them in a global, long-term vision
Symbol	An arrow, indicating direction
Key word	Which direction? Where are we going?
Archetype[†]	Apollo at Delphi – god of divination and of predicting the future
Celebrities[†]	De Gaulle, Gandhi, Martin Luther King, Leonardo da Vinci
General character traits	Faculties of concentration and conception Strength of interior images which give rise to original views of the world Expresses images in a concentrated manner; thinks in silence but so intensely that he may believe he has spoken out loud
Learning	Prefers to learn alone, by reading and taking the necessary time to deepen understanding
Problem-solving	Ability to define the long-term goal; strategic vision without getting lost in the details Able to organize the means in order to achieve the goal
Leadership	Based on the clarity of the vision and the energy expended to achieve it. Respects competence alone
Professional life	Activities requiring synthesis and design of complex systems Research, strategizing, executive leadership, systems designer
Potential risks	Can occasionally prefer theory despite facts to the contrary; neglects the external world, relationship difficulties. Can be perceived as obstinate and arrogant; at times has difficulty communicating

Table 1.4 – Introverted Sensing (Si)

Nature	Propensity to categorize, classify, and archive experiences and information and make use of previous learning
Symbol	A cube, a balanced, well-defined shape
Key word	What? What's to be done?
Archetype[†]	Hephaestus/Vulcan – god of the forge and fire
Celebrities[†]	Diderot (Encyclopédie), Sherlock Holmes, the heroine in *The Girl with a Pearl Earring* (by Tracy Chevalier) and the hero in *Perfume: The Story of a Murderer* (by Patrick Süskind), the ant in Jean de la Fontaine's fable "The Ant and the Grasshopper"
General character traits	Functions like photographic film: quietly records every little detail without reacting externally Follows the rules, procedures, any proven method Respects tradition, values stability Revisits the past to learn from it Cautiousness which can be mistaken for passivity
Learning	Learns methodically in a stable environment, following tested methods
Problem-solving	Collects quantifiable, specific data; catalogues and compares it to information stored previously Builds on what has been done earlier
Leadership	Generally respects designated authority and expects the same respect from others Likes to be decisive once sufficient information is available
Professional life	Activities requiring a methodical approach, concentration, and perseverance Managers, accountants, librarians and, in general, caretakers of the system. Logistics champions
Potential risk	Excessive emphasis on detail May feel overwhelmed by excessive responsibility Lack of flexibility, spontaneity, zest for life

Table 1.5 – Extraverted Intuiting (Ne)

Nature	Propensity to produce a constant flow of new ideas and possibilities in any situation, at any time
Symbol	A dandelion seed-head "sowing seed on the four winds"
Key word	Why not? "I bet I can…!"
Archetype[†]	Hermes/Mercury, god of communication and commerce
Celebrities[†]	Peter Pan, Jean-Paul Gaultier, Marco Polo, Perrette in Jean de la Fontaine's fable "The Milk Maid and the Milk Pail"
General character traits	Able to "stir up" ideas, be inventive Good communicator, engages easily with others, able to "sell" his ideas Adapts easily, rebounds, moves on to the next thing Quick to see "the big picture", able to see the shape of things to come, able to sense the current climate
Learning	In an interactive setting, through an effervescent bubbling of ideas and exchanges with others
Problem-solving	Highly creative, able to see "outside the box", reframe ideas innovatively, make new and original connections
Leadership	Leads through enthusiastic presentation of the vision, constantly striving to find new ideas or new ways of doing things.
Professional life	Work involving communication, entrepreneurship Traders, innovators Choses to work wherever there is a need to ensure progress, move the system forward
Potential risks	Unrealistic, may have difficulty persevering and implementing projects undertaken; difficulty meeting deadlines and following plans; Motto: "practical support to follow" Disproportionate risk-taking, instability

Table 1.6 – Extraverted Thinking (Te)

Nature	Propensity to organize and structure the environment in a logical, orderly, and efficient manner
Symbol	Lightning bolt, symbol of celestial power
Key word	Onward! Forward!
Archetype[†]	Zeus/Jupiter – king of the gods, ruler of Olympus
Celebrities[†]	Napoleon, Alexander the Great, Le Nôtre, Taylor
General character traits	Acts according to rational and logical criteria that are easily formulated Believes in the principle of cause and effect: every effect has a cause Fan of the "one best way" Plans, organizes, leads in any and all sectors of life
Learning	Learns in a logical, organized manner, with no time wasted. Enjoys challenges and competitions which require learning – winning or losing is of secondary importance
Problem-solving	Easily able to deconstruct a whole into its constituent sub-elements. Makes decisions quickly and clearly in accordance with rational, objective criteria
Leadership	Naturally occupies leadership positions Willingly shoulders authority, implements an action plan, and delegates tasks
Professional life	Often found in positions of responsibility At ease in fields governed by logic and in businesses where a mechanical model of organization prevails
Potential risks	May become a tyrant, dictating to others and imposing his method as the only one worthy Rationalizes everything, has difficulty getting in touch with feelings and expressing them

Table 1.7 – Introverted Feeling (Fi)

Nature	Propensity to create harmony around deeply felt personal values
Symbol	A flame (interior, the home hearth)
Key word	Who? For what purpose?
Archetype[†]	Hestia/Vesta – goddess sanctifying hearth and home, revered everywhere
Celebrities[†]	Audrey Hepburn, Cyrano de Bergerac, Abraham Lincoln, Abbé Pierre
General character traits	Inspires other group members through setting a strong example; values are transmitted through influence, not proselytism Likes to discover the meaning of things, their deepest signification; A dreamer, needs solitude to recharge; Creates intimacy among friends around deep subjects; Highly empathic
Learning	Needs to understand the deeper meaning of the subject being taught and have it conform to his values Requires a climate of cooperation and the freedom to explore
Problem-solving	Combines imagination and an ability seek out the new with certainty and conviction founded on ethical beliefs
Leadership	Leads more by influence than by direct authority; willingly takes on the role of "éminence grise" for someone else identified as the decision-maker
Professional life	Comfortable in a number of situations as long as there are shared values. Often found in counselling and supporting professions and wherever the interplay of human relationships is at stake.
Potential risks	May become excessively attached to values or individuals and lose objectivity Intolerance which may lead to aggressiveness May often appear cold when first encountered

Table 1.8 – Introverted Thinking (Ti)

Nature	Propensity to look for a rational explanation for everything through constant questioning and re-evaluation
Symbol	A question mark
Key word	Why? And again, why?
Archetype[†]	Prometheus, in search of fire and truth
Celebrities[†]	Socrates, Kant, Nietzsche, Jung, Einstein
General character traits	Interested in the concept, the essential nature of things Clear-sighted, critical thinker, asks questions to get to the heart of the matter Disregards nonessential concepts, notices inconsistencies Pursues in-depth analysis and does not deviate from rigorous application of reason or operational logic
Learning	Reflection and advanced study of written material Contact with subject experts Critical analysis of experience
Problem-solving	Search for the explanatory principles and the best modes of operation Arrangement of logical sequences and definition of critical pathways
Leadership	Based on the clarity of the vision of the steps to be taken and on the competence to implement them
Professional life	Particularly comfortable in the field of invention and research Oriented toward practical achievement, provides effective business leadership, with clear goals and programs.
Potential risks	Excessive questioning, overthinking, tendency to "split hairs" Difficulty expressing feelings, coldness, lack of consideration for others

Table 1.9 – Extraverted Feeling (Fe)

Nature	Propensity to be in harmony with others based on objective, shared values
Symbol	A circle (of friends, family)
Key word	Together!
Archetype[†]	Hera/Juno, keeper of commitments Demeter/Ceres, mother-goddess of the earth and harvest
Celebrities[†]	Mother Theresa, Mary Poppins, Pope Jean-Paul II, Angela Davis
General character traits	Enthusiasm, dynamism, desire to put values to work for the common good Organized, methodical, maintains close contact with others; A "people person" Focused on people, ready to help and to share
Learning	Learns through interaction with others who share the same values
Problem-solving	Focuses on what matters most to others involved Able to decide quickly and organize efforts in an orderly fashion
Leadership	Willingly accepts positions of authority and leads with charisma Leads by force of conviction and the desire to put values to work for the common good
Professional life	All people-oriented professions, particularly supporting relationships
Potential risks	Conformism, overzealousness, may want more for others than others want for themselves Clear conscience, lack of critical sense, emotional dependence

ORDER OF INTEGRATION OF THE FUNCTIONS

The eight functions do not reveal themselves in each individual's psyche in exactly the same way. They develop in a specific order which differs according to the individual's psychological type. Among the eight functions, the first two form a central core around which the others are ranked in accordance with the law of polar opposites. For this reason, we will refer to each type based on the initials of the first two functions, for example Fe/Ti to designate a person who has Extraverted Feeling as the first function and Introverted Thinking as the second function. This creates a pair of two "preferred" functions which are "preferred" not in the sense of an intentional choice, but rather as a natural predisposition or pre-existing psychic "formatting". They are like a pair of glasses which – unbeknownst to us – we are already wearing. These functions are the ones which strongly express our deepest intentions and everything that is most intrinsic to our system of values.

But everyone has all eight functions, and they all have a role to play; becoming aware of the "glasses" we are wearing is important as it will help us to change glasses when needed. The other functions, called "non-preferred functions", all establish themselves in the course of each individual's development, but they each follow a different path and begin to appear at different stages of life. As in nature, where some flowers bloom in spring or summer, so also do we observe each function grow and flourish throughout the course of our life. This occurs in the following order, and will be illustrated with two contrasting examples:

- Joseph, Te/Si, Extraverted Thinking/Introverted Sensing, and
- Olivia, Fi/Ne, Introverted Feeling/Extraverted Intuiting.

As we describe the developing functions, they will be indicated on the "function cross" for Joseph and for Olivia.

It is important to note that psychological type can be indicated in two different ways:

- either by using the two primary functions (dominant and auxiliary), which reflects the dynamic of the type,
- or by using the four letters indicating preference on the four opposing poles of the cross (E/I, S/N, T/F, J/P); this latter system is generally used for personality type indicators.

We will use the dominant/auxiliary designation, followed by the 4-letter code equivalent in parentheses.

The functions are described as being "light" or "shadow" according to whether they are preferred by an individual or not. In fact, if I position myself where things appear to be in the light, the other functions are in shadow, blurry, inaccessible, even negative. But for another person, these same functions will be light, whereas my preferred functions may be the other's shadow. As well, I will at times be able to shed light on my shadow functions, and project this light to see what new things the shadow functions can contribute.

The "Light" Functions – Dominant and Auxiliary

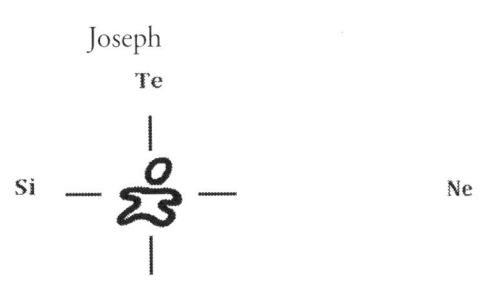

Figure 1.1 – Joseph's Light functions: Te/Si (Extraverted Thinking/ Introverted Sensing)

Figure 1.2 – Olivia's Light functions: Fi/Ne (Introverted Feeling/ Extraverted Intuiting)

Dominant Function

This is the psyche's organizing function; it is the first in several ways.

It manifests itself from the start of one's psychic life, as early as infancy. For example, with Joseph and Olivia:

- Extraverted Thinking (Te), Joseph's dominant function, expresses a spontaneous tendency to organize the universe; Joseph's nickname as a child was "captain" (as a matter of fact, other individuals of this type often admit to nicknames such as "boss", "commander", or "general").
- Introverted Feeling (Fi), Olivia's dominant function, is oriented towards an inner values quest; Olivia's favorite subject in elementary school was civics education, and later, ethics.

The dominant function is the one that we tend to resort to first and spontaneously to solve a problem or to deal with an unexpected situation:

- At the start of an organized trip, Joseph, a participant like the others, immediately takes on a leadership role at the airport, promptly proposing a communal "kitty" for the group's minor expenses.
- At the same time, Olivia begins by quietly observing the group members to get an idea of who they are; she also watches for the conclusion of the "social grooming"[5] and the chance to form new relationships.

The dominant function is also the one used the most skillfully, or the most easily, relatively speaking. However, this doesn't mean that the dominant function is always used well. It's possible to have Thinking as the dominant function and spout nonsense; or Feeling as dominant, and have a skewed values system; or Sensing as dominant, and collect trivia; or Intuition as dominant and be out in left field!

This preference may have been encouraged by the surrounding environment from earliest infancy, and the child thus develops with

---

[5] Expression inspired by studies in ethnology, designating conversation preliminaries. See for example *The Naked Ape*, by Desmond Morris, 1968.

great confidence. He feels loved unconditionally, for being himself. This gives the child a very solid basis for self-esteem, confidence, and healthy differentiation to develop.

The opposite can also occur and in that case, the child cannot understand why he is criticized each time his dominant function expresses itself. He is rebuked, mocked, or possibly worse, ignored. As a result, he will either have to abandon his identity, with the resultant frustrations, or resist and pay the price, or alternate between these two strategies. His self-concept will suffer from this, and he may spend a long time wondering what he did wrong until he discovers that his preferences were simply not viewed favorably in his birth family. The story of the "Ugly Duckling" exemplifies this.

> Extraverted Joseph suffered enormously from not being able to go out to see his friends as often as he would have liked, but his parents brought him up to believe that it was just not acceptable to spend all his time with his friends. He suffered considerable loneliness until he moved away to university and could live the life that suited him.
>
> Olivia, on the other hand, often felt like staying in her room, particularly as she had many siblings, but her extraverted parents constantly pushed her to participate in extracurricular activities and to be more social, which she found worrisome, until she was able to live alone and do as she liked.

Auxiliary Function

The auxiliary function counterbalances the dominant function in two ways:

- the auxiliary will be a Perceiving function if the dominant is Judging, and vice versa;
- the auxiliary will be an introverted function ("i") if the dominant is extraverted ("e"), and vice versa;

The concept of balancing is essential, just as a sailboat must have both a rudder and sails.

- If it has only a rudder (Judging function), there will be a clear direction, but the boat will not move.
- If it has only sails, (Perceiving function), it will certainly move, but it will float aimlessly in all directions.
- It is of utmost importance to take into consideration both our inner and outer experiences; one of the two principal functions takes charge of the outer world, and the other the inner world. The transition from reflection to action will facilitate the back-and-forth movement between Perceiving and Judging, and thus between information-gathering and decision-making.

The auxiliary function really comes into its own in the period around adolescence, and in this way it expands our psychic identity as it enables us to access a function which is in every way the complete opposite of our dominant function.

It is generally easy to use this function, as it is close to the dominant function.

> Joseph, whose auxiliary function is Introverted Sensing (Si), is very practical in his approach. He is dying to take on the responsibility for the communal kitty. Moreover, proof of his organizational skills shows up in tangible results: he is an amateur photographer whose slide collection is catalogued perfectly; as well, having created a training center, he oversees the work site in such a way that no detail escapes his attention.
>
> Olivia, whose auxiliary function is Extraverted Intuiting (Ne), exhibits a constant curiosity for personal development projects. Her search for meaning (Fi) is evident in the realm of personal relationships, spiritual and psychological development, and everything that "connects".

Table 1.10 shows the 16 possible combinations of the eight functions, in light of the rules described above.

Table 1.10 – The 16 Types

Function	Type	Dominant function	Auxiliary function
Se/Ti	ESTP	Extraverted Sensing	Introverted Thinking
Se/Fi	ESFP	Extraverted Sensing	Introverted Feeling
Si/Te	ISTJ	Introverted Sensing	Extraverted Thinking
Si/Fe	ISFJ	Introverted Sensing	Extraverted Feeling
Ne/Ti	ENTP	Extraverted Intuiting	Introverted Thinking
Ne/Fi	ENFP	Extraverted Intuiting	Introverted Feeling
Ni/Te	INTJ	Introverted Intuiting	Extraverted Thinking
Ni/Fe	INFJ	Introverted Intuiting	Extraverted Feeling
Te/Si	ESTJ	Extraverted Thinking	Introverted Sensing
Te/Ni	ENTJ	Extraverted Thinking	Introverted Intuiting
Ti/Se	ISTP	Introverted Thinking	Extraverted Sensing
Ti/Ne	INTP	Introverted Thinking	Extraverted Intuiting
Fe/Si	ESFJ	Extraverted Feeling	Introverted Sensing
Fe/Ni	ENFJ	Extraverted Feeling	Introverted Intuiting
Fi/Se	ISFP	Introverted Feeling	Extraverted Sensing
Fi/Ne	INFP	Introverted Feeling	Extraverted Intuiting

The Shadow: Tertiary and Inferior Functions

The function crosses for Joseph and Olivia can be completed as follows

Joseph

```
       Te
       |
Si ─── ✱ ─── Ne
       |
       Fi
```

Olivia

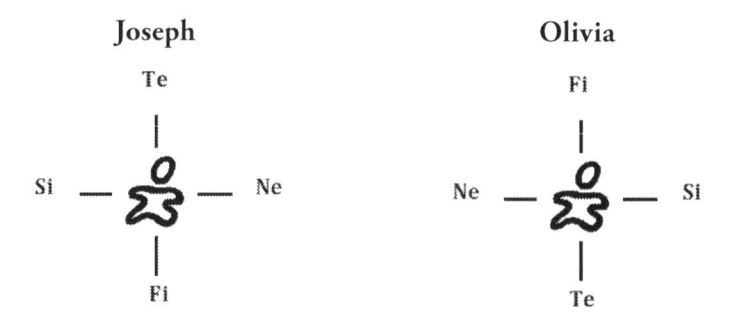

```
       Fi
       |
Ne ─── ✱ ─── Si
       |
       Te
```

Figure 1.3 – Joseph's shadow functions: Fi/Ne (Introverted Feeling/Extraverted Intuiting)

Figure 1.4 – Olivia's shadow functions: Te/Si (Extraverted Thinking/Introverted Sensing)

Tertiary Function

This is the pole which is opposite the auxiliary in the same dimension, but with an opposite orientation.

The tertiary function develops at the beginning of adulthood, often due to environmental pressures which require us to adapt to new situations.

> As he was given more important responsibilities, Joseph was required to face unforeseen circumstances. He found that he had to relax his rather strict organizational style in order to be more highly regarded. He had to incorporate more teamwork and consultation and be more willing to call on the skills and knowledge of his team members. In this way, ideas he had not considered were brought forward; they were well accepted by all team members, and this was extremely motivating, particularly for Joseph. His tertiary function, Extraverted Intuiting (Ne), was thus able to contribute in a strong way. These kinds of procedures do not slow him down any more, and he is able to get around them when necessary. A process which he viewed as a waste of time proved to be effective.

For Olivia, everything related to practical matters (schedules, administrative forms, routine daily activities) was pure torture and she often procrastinated, postponing these tasks indefinitely, until her professional or family responsibilities led her to call on her Introverted Sensing (Si) function; having done this, she learned to enjoy the resultant benefits (comfort and security).

The tertiary function is more difficult to incorporate and slower to access than the two preferred functions, and therefore, it manifests in a similar way to the inferior function, which we will now look at more closely

Inferior Function

This is the pole opposite the dominant in the same dimension, but with an opposite orientation.

The inferior function generally develops midway through life and occasionally in an abrupt or dramatic manner, particularly if we have overlooked or suppressed its qualities for too long. It is not just a coincidence that we speak of the "midlife crisis".

The inferior function often manifests in the problems it can cause:

- inconsistency:
    - through insufficiency or lack: it appears completely absent, or
    - through excess: there is indiscriminate zealousness.

    This is why Olivia, who has Extraverted Thinking as her inferior function, often has difficulty with aspects of pure logic. She needs time to put the concepts into writing (Si) and she doesn't like to be rushed. Caught up in sensations which are difficult to articulate, she has difficulty stating her thoughts in a clear and unemotional way. Until the moment when, her cup overflowing with unexpressed feelings, she explodes, surprising herself most of all and putting herself at odds with others around her

- tactlessness, verbal awkwardness

    Joseph, whose inferior function is Introverted Feeling (Fi), has difficulty expressing affection in any way other than in the form of jokes or teasing, or even mockery, which can be difficult for others to interpret

- touchiness, irritability

    Don't try to tell Robert, Ni/Te, who has Extraverted Sensing as his inferior function, that he has once again made mistakes in taking the measurements for a construction project. He is already upset enough as it is!

The inferior function is a reservoir of untapped potential and the starting point for self-development.

> Through the years, Olivia has progressively taken on a more and more important role in her company, and she is currently very pleased to find herself putting her significant talents to great effect in an executive position, which is entirely typical for Extraverted Thinking. She is able to appreciate the progress she has made.
>
> As for Joseph, he is currently pursuing a career in the field of individual coaching, where his empathy, typical of Introverted Feeling, is every bit as sought after and effective as organizational skills.

In Praise of Deliberation: "The Night Brings Counsel"

The two non-preferred functions, the tertiary and the inferior, are far from being nonexistent. They are just less accessible than the others. The simple measure of taking some time – when making a decision, for example – enables these two functions to arise in the field of consciousness. "The night brings counsel", or so we say. Why? It is the time when the two preferred functions, which reign our waking hours, slacken their efforts and let the others come to the fore. How many inventions and realizations are the fruit of these "passive" hours? Sleep facilitates a natural rebalancing.

The Shadow of the Shadow, or the "Opposite" Functions

In practice, it is common to limit the description to the roles of the first four functions. Being able to differentiate between these four is already a significant achievement! However, the four other "opposite" functions truly exist in the psyche, and we will have the opportunity to see some of their displays.

The "opposite" functions are the same ones described above, but in the opposite orientation. For example, if the dominant function is Introverted Sensing, then the dominant in the opposite orientation is Extraverted Sensing. These are the most unconscious functions, the ones that are the most difficult to access. They are called the "opposite" functions.

Being familiar with these "opposite" functions will enable us to better understand the mechanisms of projection, which will be discussed later on.

The order of the eight functions for Joseph, Te/Si, and Olivia, Fi/Ne, is indicated below. A similar cross can be drawn for each of the 16 types. Table 1.11 shows the order of the functions for each of the 16 types.

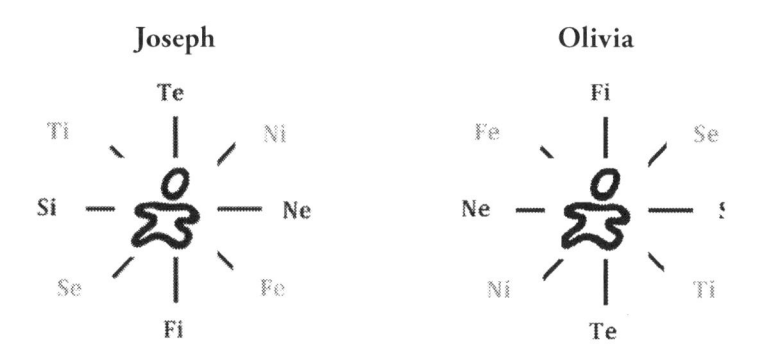

Figure 1.5 – "Opposite" functions for type Te/Si (Extraverted Thinking/Introverted Feeling)

Figure 1.6 – "Opposite" functions for type Fi/Ne (Introverted Feeling/Extraverted Intuiting)

Table 1.11 shows the order of the eight functions for each one of the 16 possible combinations or personality types.

Table 1.11 – Order of the Functions

Si/Te (ISTJ)	Si/Fe (ISFJ)	Ni/Fe (INFJ)	Ni/Te (INTJ)
Introverted Sensing Extraverted Thinking Introverted Feeling Extraverted Intuiting Extraverted Sensing Introverted Thinking Extraverted Feeling Introverted Intuiting	Introverted Sensing Extraverted Feeling Introverted Thinking Extraverted Intuiting Extraverted Sensing Introverted Feeling Extraverted Thinking Introverted Intuiting	Introverted Intuiting Extraverted Feeling Introverted Thinking Extraverted Sensing Extraverted Intuiting Introverted Feeling Extraverted Thinking Introverted Sensing	Introverted Intuiting Extraverted Thinking Introverted Feeling Extraverted Sensing Extraverted Intuiting Introverted Thinking Extraverted Feeling Introverted Sensing
Ti/Se (ISTP)	**Fi/Se (ISFP)**	**Fi/Ne (INFP)**	**Ti/Ne (INTP)**
Introverted Thinking Extraverted Sensing Introverted Intuiting Extraverted Feeling Extraverted Thinking Introverted Sensing Extraverted Intuiting Introverted Feeling	Introverted Feeling Extraverted Sensing Introverted Intuiting Extraverted Thinking Extraverted Feeling Introverted Sensing Extraverted Intuiting Introverted Thinking	Introverted Feeling Extraverted Intuiting Introverted Sensing Extraverted Thinking Extraverted Feeling Introverted Intuiting Extraverted Sensing Introverted Thinking	Introverted Thinking Extraverted Intuiting Introverted Sensing Extraverted Feeling Extraverted Thinking Introverted Intuiting Extraverted Sensing Introverted Feeling
Se/Ti (ESTP)	**Se/Fi (ESFP)**	**Ne/Fi (ENFP)**	**Ne/Ti (ENTP)**
Extraverted Sensing Introverted Thinking Extraverted Feeling Introverted Intuiting Introverted Sensing Extraverted Thinking Introverted Feeling Extraverted Intuiting	Extraverted Sensing Introverted Feeling Extraverted Thinking Introverted Intuiting Introverted Sensing Extraverted Feeling Introverted Thinking Extraverted Intuiting	Extraverted Intuiting Introverted Feeling Extraverted Thinking Introverted Sensing Introverted Intuiting Extraverted Feeling Introverted Thinking Extraverted Sensing	Extraverted Intuiting Introverted Thinking Extraverted Feeling Introverted Sensing Introverted Intuiting Extraverted Thinking Introverted Feeling Extraverted Sensing
Te/Si (ESTJ)	**Fe/Si (ESFJ)**	**Fe/Ni (ENFJ)**	**Te/Ni (ENTJ)**
Extraverted Thinking Introverted Sensing Extraverted Intuiting Introverted Feeling Introverted Thinking Extraverted Sensing Introverted Intuiting Extraverted Feeling	Extraverted Feeling Introverted Sensing Extraverted Intuiting Introverted Thinking Introverted Feeling Extraverted Sensing Introverted Intuiting Extraverted Thinking	Extraverted Feeling Introverted Intuiting Extraverted Sensing Introverted Thinking Introverted Feeling Extraverted Intuiting Introverted Sensing Extraverted Thinking	Extraverted Thinking Introverted Intuiting Extraverted Sensing Introverted Feeling Introverted Thinking Extraverted Intuiting Introverted Sensing Extraverted Feeling

In summary

From birth, we have available to us eight fundamental processes which enable us to relate to and interact with our environment, collect information, and make decisions. These processes form opposing pairs; we make use of all eight, but we spontaneously call on one pair more easily. Accessing the other pair requires more effort, and we learn to use it over the course of our life.

Whatever our natural tendencies may be, we must develop strategies which enable us to meet the demands that work, personal life, and family place upon us. How that occurs is the topic of the next chapter.

2

SPONTANEOUS EVOLUTION OF THE PSYCHE: THE AUTO-PILOT (OR OPERATING EGO)

ADAPTATION STRATEGIES

Origins

The spontaneous cognitive processes which we have just discussed form the basic matrix of our psyche, which is endowed with plasticity to adapt to its environment. Based on our needs, we learn to adopt the most appropriate behaviors, given our capabilities. In this way, we develop adaptation strategies which become progressively more prominent in the psyche as they prove their effectiveness.

Adaptation begins very early: we use our first strategies with the intent of satisfying our hunger. An infant will quickly discover the most efficient means of getting its mother's attention or a bottle within the familial context: it will smile, cry, scream, or not ask for anything at all, or use another strategy.

We continue to develop new strategies throughout our life. The same general objective may, in fact, require several different strategies depending on our surroundings: if our goal is getting approval, we don't approach a parent, a teacher, or a classmate in the same way.

This explains how Mom's "little angel" at home can become a little devil at school, and vice versa, or how the tyrannical employer turns out to be a "teddy bear" at home, and vice versa.

Overview of the Strategies

The dominant or primary strategies are the ones that have been successful for the individual from the start. They bring into play a complete repertory of behaviors, body language, thoughts, and emotions, which are easily recognized as energy schemas. Just like a diamond, we are all composed of a countless number of facets, or parts, each different from the others. These parts do not look alike, they do not use the same vocabulary, they do not reason in the same way, nor do they deal with people in a similar fashion.

Unlike the psychic functions, the number of strategies one individual can rely on is unlimited. There may even be several strategies depending on the range of environments in which we find ourselves. Based on our experience, however, we find that often two or three preferred strategies emerge from the group and occupy the majority of the terrain. The "Pareto principle" can be applied here as well, whereby 20% of our primary behavioral strategies are responsible for 80% of our psychic activity!

Every individual's strategies are unique. There are common characteristics from one individual to the next, but the strength of the strategy lies in its uniqueness. The groups of strategies shown below are simply guidelines, a starting point – all individuals will need to discover their own patterns of behavior, as only then will they be able to understand themselves and evolve.

As we all share common environments, it is not surprising that we find groups of strategies that we each make use of in a very unique way. Here then, are some of the most common groups of strategies, at least in the economic, social, and cultural context of our Western world.

Becoming Who You Are with the Intelligence of Self

Table 2.1 – Adaptation Strategies

Contribution Why the strategy is originally established	Limitations When the strategy becomes excessive
The Inner Child	
The Inner Child is not, strictly speaking, a strategy. It is the Self's most vulnerable part; it is the most intimate and the most sensitive. It is very close to the soul. It needs an environment which feels safe in order to manifest. Without an Inner Child, one cannot form an intimate relationship with oneself or with others; there can be no spiritual life. We quickly feel omnipotent.	When the Inner Child oversteps its bounds, the individual may become too impulsive or behave in an infantile manner. It may appear overly spontaneous and naïve, all the while protesting that it is "frank and sincere" The individual may easily feel victimized or play the spoiled "child-king".
The Protector	
The Protector takes up his place to take care of the child. It is the armor that protects the child from difficulties and injury. It knows the rules of the social game and enables the individual to act in an appropriate manner. Without the Protector, the child is soon overwhelmed or becomes maladjusted.	When the Protector oversteps his bounds, the individual may become rigid, not expressing feelings or emotions, or may present an insensitive façade. It may avoid any situation where there is the slightest risk of the Inner Child being exposed, which makes any type of intimate relationship impossible.
The Rule Maker	
The Rule Maker proclaims the laws and rules arising in the Auto-Pilot. It indicates good and evil, and the principles governing a moral life. These rules differ depending on whether the Auto-Pilot is allied with Thinking or Feeling. Without the Rule Maker, it is not possible to live in social groups.	The Rule Maker is quick to wrap itself in self-righteousness and virtue. When it oversteps its bounds, the individual may become intolerant, moralizing, ponti-ficating. It has harsh judgments for those who do not adhere to the same rules. The Rule Maker can easily start religious wars, even when preaching tolerance!

The Perfectionist	
The Perfectionist sets very high standards for determining success. One of its mottos could be "You who have declared 'That's good enough', you are already dead'". (St Augustine†) It always pushes the individual to do better, to extend the limits. Without the Perfectionist, there would be no great achievements in art, science, or any field.	The unfettered Perfectionist drives the individual to exhaustion, depression, and despair. Nothing is ever good enough; there is always an improvement to make; one can always do better. At a certain level, the Perfectionist impedes progress, because nothing is ever good enough to be considered finished.

The Inner Critic	
The Inner Critic is the policeman who signals all infractions of the rules. It proclaims each and every lapse, error, imperfection, or inadequacy. It is the strong arm of the Rule Maker. It often has a lofty idea of an individual's potential and reminds him of it. Without the cricket perched on Pinocchio's shoulder, there is no awakening of one's conscience.	An unrestrained Inner Critic can systematically and mercilessly chastise the individual and ruin his life. Allied with the Perfectionist, the Inner Critic can drive us quickly to lose self-confidence, dragging us into a downward spiral of failure, regardless of our actual successes and achievements.

The Patriarch/The Matriarch	
These are the inner voices, acquired culturally, that determine the social roles of men and women: – the Patriarch is the masculine authority figure which gives the feminine its place in society; – the Matriarch is the feminine authority figure which gives the masculine its place in society. These voices take on the responsibility for ensuring the stability of the social structure.	The Patriarch and the Matriarch can quickly overstep their position. They often become very vocal at the time of a marriage or the birth of a first child, even in a "liberated" or "evolved" couple. And so the Patriarch strives to put the female under male domination and reminds her of her obligations toward him. In turn, the Matriarch strives to put the male under female domination and reminds him of his obligations toward her. In Western cultures, the Patriarch has largely gained the upper hand, and there are numerous signs of this excess, to the great detriment of the balance between the sexes.

The Caretaker	
The Caretaker strives to be a good parent, to take care of its children – and its own Inner Child. The Caretaker tends to help others spontaneously, with the same loving kindness, even when the others are no longer children. Without the Caretaker, children could not survive, or would barely scrape by. "Man would be a wolf to man" (Plautus†), and charitable organizations would undoubtedly not exist.	The individual whose Caretaker oversteps the bounds tends to forget himself, like the pelican who sacrifices itself for its young (Alfred de Musset†). In the extreme, this individual tries to do good for others despite their own wishes, like the young Scout who, attempting to do a good deed, helps a blind man cross a road against his wishes. This person would rather do the fishing rather than teach another to fish.

The Responsible	
The Responsible has a sense of duty and a clear idea of the task to be accomplished. This leads one to become a good professional who can be relied upon. Without the voice of responsibility, scholarly or professional success is difficult.	Taken to excess, the Responsible becomes a "workaholic" who puts work ahead of everything else. These individuals can thus forget their private lives and the existence of the Inner Child. In retirement, workaholics either keep busy or fall into a depression.

THE AUTO-PILOT (THE OPERATING EGO)

Characteristics

As the child develops, some ways of doing things are more successful than others; circuits are created in the brain, and habits are learned. The child's personality is formed through a process of favoring certain tendencies and banishing others to the shadow.

Neuroscience clearly describes this cerebral plasticity. Neural networks change their synaptic connections, and this therefore impacts their organization. This process occurs in two ways:

- unconsciously, depending on the type of experiences the person has undergone. The brain will:
    - either solidify the connections which proved effective in achieving results and which are associated with pleasure; these specific synapses are reinforced and their capacity increases,
    - or eliminate the connections which have proven to be ineffective or which are associated with negative emotions; these specific synapses are thus neutralized, and they lose their "charge" like a dead battery;
- intentionally, to develop strategies which contrast with the existing ones. This requires the brain to undergo the following changes:
    - a disruption at the synapse level,
    - a loss of some of the previous information, and
    - a reorganization around new connections, which does not entail a general loss of coherence.

This process occurs as if new highways were being built, and a number of "secondary" lanes were simply abandoned. When these new lanes start to be more heavily traveled, it becomes essential to rebuild and improve the traffic signals.

We will therefore start by looking at these "highways", or rather the Auto-Pilot, also called the Operating Ego, and its spontaneous evolution.

In the next chapter, we will look at how we can improve the traffic signals of the new lanes and undertake an "intelligent process of becoming", resulting in a broader range of options available to us.

Creation of the Operating Ego

The interaction between the strategies required by our environment and the developing psychic processes gives rise to the creation of Sub-Personalities, otherwise known as "Parts" or "Selves". Each Part is created in reaction to a presenting vulnerability where the Part steps in to protect and assist us in dealing with a particular situation by adopting certain strategies or behaviors. We speak of primary Sub-Personalities to show that they are not only first in order of appearance, but also first in terms of their importance in our psychic life.

The complete set of primary Sub-Personalities forms the Operating Ego or the Auto-Pilot. Although the number of strategies, and thus the number of Sub-Personalities, is in theory unlimited, in practice it can be seen that the Auto-Pilot is usually composed of two or three Sub-Personalities, with just one of them often playing the largest role.

The Operating Ego may take on several forms.

To use a musical analogy, the strategies are the written scores for each different instrument, and the processes are the instrument. A melody is not played the same way from one instrument to the next; some musical pieces are better adapted to one instrument than another, or they are more often played on one instrument than another.

To illustrate this in another way, in the computer technology field, the functions are the "hardware", the way in which the computer processes information, and the strategies are the "software" in use. Some types of software function better on one specific computer than on another, or require a patch or adaptation to function well.

There are two main types of interactions between the functions and the strategies. The strategies required by the environment:

- correspond to fundamental psychic processes, to the first two functions; and
- call to mind one or more shadow functions.

We will use the function cross and give some examples of the different interactions.

Strategies and Preferred Functions

We will start with the example of Robert, Ni/Te (INTJ) – Introverted Intuiting/Extraverted Thinking.

"The idea factory" (Ni/Te)

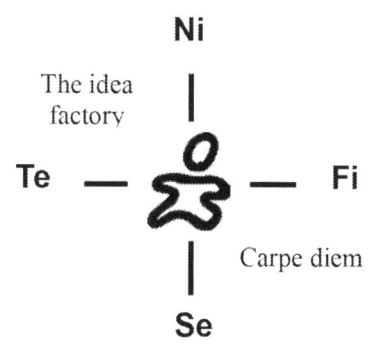

Figure 2.1 – Function Cross Ni/Te (Introverted Intuiting/Extraverted Thinking)

Robert learned very early in childhood that success at school was a necessity, even an absolute must, not to be taken lightly, and this idea was transmitted with his first baby bottle.

This fundamental strategy of "success through intellectual competency" falls on fertile ground. Statistically speaking, the type INTJ has the best success in school. In Robert's case, things turn out so well that he gets caught up in the game without even realizing it. Introverted Intuiting, his dominant function, is a magnificent source of ideas. Extraverted Thinking, his auxiliary function, doesn't stop until it has created everything it imagines. It is not surprising that at one point in his life, Robert juggles three jobs. His lifestyle could be summed up in this pastiche[6]: "What is

---

[6] BOILEAU, *Art poétique*. « Ce que l'on conçoit bien s'énonce clairement/Et les mots pour le dire arrivent aisément. » *(Transl. "Whatever we well understand we express clearly/And words flow with ease.")*

well understood is clearly stated/And the subsequent actions easy to achieve". Robert works like a donkey at the watermill, round and round, unable to stop.

With experience, we have observed that there is an "affinity" between certain strategies and functions. Table 2.2 provides some correlations which can actually be deduced based on the description given earlier of the eight functions.

Table 2.2 – Functions and Strategies

Function	Strategy
Extraverted Sensing (Se)	The problem-solver: "There is always a solution."
Introverted Sensing (Si)	The expert: "There is always a method."
Extraverted Intuiting (Ne)	The explorer: "It's a new world out there every morning."
Introverted Intuiting (Ni)	The strategist: "The future is now."
Extraverted Thinking (Te)	The organizer: "This is the right way."
Introverted Thinking (Ti)	The inquisitor: "Why?"
Extraverted Feeling (Fe)	The caretaker: "It's for your own good."
Introverted Feeling (Fi)	The bearer of meaning: "Which way do we go?"

Observations:

- Care should be taken to avoid interpreting this table as if it were a key that opened all locks; these are simply some general links corresponding to a wide range of different situations.
- In practice, as is the case for Robert shown above, there will be combinations of the two preferred functions and the necessary strategies.

Strategies and Shadow Functions

It is also possible for the Auto-Pilot to call on a shadow function, particularly the tertiary function, which has the same orientation as the dominant. In this case, it can be excessive. Two cases are possible.

Alliance Dominant/Tertiary Functions

"The Fighter" (NeTe)

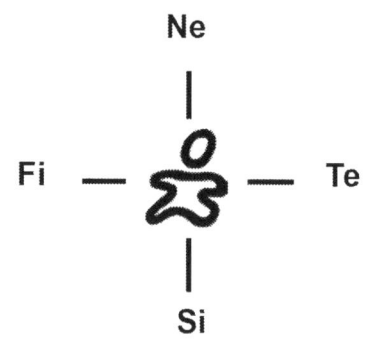

Ne

Fi — — **Te**

Si

Figure 2.2 – Function Cross Ne/Fi (Extraverted Intuiting/Introverted Feeling)

Born into a family of small-business owners, Louise, Ne/Fi, Extraverted Intuiting/Introverted Feeling, is very active and aspires to achieve professional success in a large industrial enterprise. This requires not only solid grades but also a significant investment in her field, which is all the more important because, as a woman, she must unfortunately "do more to prove her competency", to restate the observation made by Françoise Giroud.[†] Her dominant function, Extraverted Intuiting (Ne), is completely appropriate for creating this dynamic, but the auxiliary function, Introverted Feeling (Fi), is not particularly valued in business as it is seen as "too feminine". It is therefore her tertiary function, Extraverted Thinking, culturally seen as "masculine", that is likely to develop earlier, as if anticipating the need, with the resultant risk of reinforcing her extraversion and minimizing her Feeling function, which would otherwise counterbalance it. In this way, the bedrock of her personality develops – she is very effective in a professional capacity – she is "a fighter", but she is at risk for burnout, and for a time she is out of touch with her inner world

Alliance Auxiliary/Inferior Functions

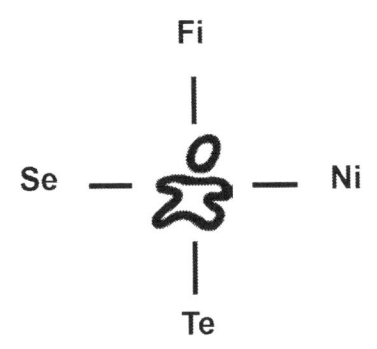

Figure 2.3 – Function Cross Fi/Se (Introverted Feeling/Extraverted Sensing)

Charles, a 40-year-old telecommunications engineer, whose type is Fi/Se, Introverted Feeling/Extraverted Sensing, feels like changing career directions completely. He wants to become a human resources consultant. This wish unsettles him, as it makes him wonder if he has wasted his time up to now, although he has had an excellent managerial career. Nonetheless, the idea interests him because he feels like he is getting back to his calling. His story is easy to piece together: good at math, the son of an engineer, Charles wanted to please (doubtless the role of Introverted Feeling) and achieve everything that was expected of him. Thus he developed quite a strategy as "the good student", and this worked for a while, but it left him at age 40 feeling frustrated and dissatisfied.

It will be noted in these examples that it is the extraverted side that tends to override the introverted side. Although we have seen some cases where the introverted side overrides the extraverted side, it appears that the two situations described above are the most common. There is a very good reason for that: the adaptation strategy is established in relation to the surrounding environment and has almost necessarily an extraverted side. The need for introversion comes later in life, when an individual feels a desire for finding a better balance.

THE THREE LAWS OF NATURAL EVOLUTION

So we find ourselves equipped with our Auto-Pilot (or Operating Ego). This is absolutely essential, as the Auto-Pilot is the one that usually conducts our daily life and enables us to dispense with reinventing the wheel every day! It has proven its effectiveness in many situations – or at any rate, it has helped us live, or survive up to now, which is already quite something.

However, what would happen if we left things entirely up to the Auto-Pilot? Without any voluntary action on our part, it would follow its own momentum, in an entropic fashion, and would develop according to three great laws:

- the law of polarization,
- the law of inflation, and
- the law of projection.

The Law of Polarization

As soon as there is an interaction between two poles, there is a constant risk of a dominant/dominated relationship – in other words, a risk of one pole taking precedence or overpowering the other completely.

Any duality imposes an unconscious choice. It is impossible to be on land and in the water, in the light and in the shadow at the same time. It is possible to do this consecutively but not simultaneously. An electric current requires a positive pole and a negative pole, but if you touch the metal pliers you are holding to the car battery terminals, you will get quite an unpleasant surprise, or at the very least, a nasty shock! Psychic energy concentrates first at one pole, then moves to the other.

The need to begin at one pole rather than the other is not a neutral choice. The half-full glass and the half-empty glass are different, even if at one point in time their contents are identical. But one is in the process of being filled, the other, being emptied; the meaning is different.

This law of polarization illustrates the nature of the Operating Ego. It is not everything all at once – it cannot be so. Our psychic structure would not exist if it were undifferentiated, and it cannot differentiate from both sides at the same time. We have to start from one side or the other, but we can start only from the one side.

This does not mean that the other side is impossible or infeasible. On the contrary, the goal of this entire process is precisely that – to enable us to access all of our potential. But we do not have the same degree of facility with both poles. With the Operating Ego, things are easy, automatic, we don't need to think twice: it's like a pre-set radio station. At the opposite pole, which we will discuss, things are more difficult – we must be attentive, put forth a greater effort, like a new radio station that we need to search for and tune into. It represents a change from the usual routine.

Here is a simple experiment which you can do as you read this:

- Cross your arms.
- Good. Now check which arm is crossed under and which is crossed over.
- Now, uncross your arms and cross them again in the opposite manner.
- Aha – not so easy, is it! And in fact, are you sure that your arms are actually crossed and not just placed with one overlapping the other?

The Operating Ego functions in the same way. It leads to a spontaneous, automatic approach. By contrast, the opposite approach requires time and a period of reflection. There is no right or wrong way to cross one's arms and, particularly if we are clear about our natural preference, we can all, with a little effort, learn to change our approach deliberately.

The Law of Inflation

There is a saying: "Don't change it if it ain't broke", and it is true – you don't make changes on a winning team. Force of habit, our growing skill, and our inability to comprehend the usefulness of the opposite pole are some factors which, compounded, result in our tendency to use the most natural strategies. This means that our behavior patterns (Auto-Pilot) become highways, and we have less and less courage to trail blaze on the small side roads. The paths and habits that we like are more fully developed than the ones we don't like. There is a self-fulfilling prophecy[7] associated with our Sub-Personalities: we expect the most from the ones that work the best and that we use the most often.

As a result, the Operating Ego tends to do more and more, even when (or maybe especially when) its approach is no longer appropriate. Right from the start, we are mired in an impressive vicious circle, similar to the individual who is told by his doctor that if the prescription isn't working, he should double the dose, or the believer whose prayer failed because his faith was not strong enough.

There is a story about a drunkard who, having dropped his key as he was opening his door, sets about looking for it under a lamppost 30 feet away from the door. When his neighbor takes him to task, he replies undauntedly "I'm looking for it where there is light".

> Zoe is type Fe/Si (ESFJ) Extraverted Feeling/Introverted Sensing. Her Auto-Pilot pushes her to always give to others, even if it means self-sacrifice. She is very reliable and generous. When unemployed, gravely ill, and confined to bed, she refuses to apply for unemployment benefits because "...in this situation, I'm not exactly unemployed, because I couldn't really work anyway". When she is told that she is giving up a benefit owed to her, and that if she were working she would be entitled to sick leave, she answers "There are so many people who cheat that someone has to be willing to restore the balance".

---

[7] In education, seeing our expectations (good and bad) met by students is called a "self-fulfilling prophecy".

In actual fact, it's not Zoe refusing the unemployment benefits. It's her Auto-Pilot which, however respectable and even admirable it may be, is no longer able to stop, and which leads her to do too much, without looking out for her own interests, and this puts her at risk for complete exhaustion.

The Law of Projection

At this point, two interlinked phenomena appear:

- Judging: The dominant pole, perfectly self-righteous, makes generally negative judgments about the opposite pole. A separation occurs in this case between "being right/being wrong". This split is both internal and external. Since we are unable to appreciate the opposite pole within us, we are critical of those who display it outwardly.
- Projection: This occurs when we project onto others the qualities (or more commonly, the faults) which we do not wish to see in ourselves. We lend them the aspects of ourselves that we dislike or of which we are unaware.

Judging and projection can be identified by the emotional intensity that accompanies them. The person who is the object of our judgment or projection generally does not merit "either the great honor, or the shame"[8]. The simple fact of observing a negative behavior and drawing conclusions from it is not necessarily a projection if we remain capable of discernment. It is when we go to extremes, when we oversimplify, when we are unable to consider opposing points of view that a red flag is raised for us. We will return to the topic of projection in more detail, as it can awaken an awareness that is of significant help in our personal development.

In this way, the dominant polarity which is the starting point for our psychic growth can become an obstacle: the system slowly begins to "seize up" and become rigid or sclerotic, restricting or preventing the flexibility required to adapt to the changing environment. By dint of plowing our path in life, we end up buried!

---

[8] RACINE[†], *Britannicus,* Act 2, scene 3

A TURF WAR

The development of the Operating Ego, or Auto-Pilot, thus leads us, by simple entropy, to disown, or push into the shadow the opposite poles, and they become the basis for the "Unintegrated Self". We will look at this more closely from the same two symmetrical viewpoints as we did to define the Operating Ego; these are:

- the Sub-Personalities, in contrast with the primary Sub-Personalities, or the unintegrated Sub-Personalities, and
- the mapping of these Sub-Personalities on the function cross.

Unintegrated Sub-Personalities

By this we mean the opposite poles of the preferred or primary polarities which have not yet been integrated into the psyche. So there are clearly as many unintegrated Sub-Personalities as there are primary Sub-Personalities.

We can identify three types of strategies or unintegrated Sub-Personalities. They are:

- unknown,
- rejected/disowned, or
- demonic.

Unknown Sub-Personalities

These are the poles opposite to the primary Sub-Personalities, and we are still unaware of them. We simply haven't experienced them yet. For example, someone brought up in a peaceful household can remain unaware of a Warrior Sub-Personality without having necessarily rejected it. It simply hasn't been needed up this point. The day we are required to fight for our life, this side may awaken, unless, in the absence of an Aware Ego, the Peace Maker part prevents the individual from accessing the Warrior.

In this way, the Internal Patriarch can remain hidden from a woman's awareness for a long time, and until 25 or 30 years of age, she behaves as a true professional, on equal footing with men. But given the demands of her biological clock, marriage, and particularly the first child, the Patriarch snaps out of its lethargy and takes an even stronger hold over its victim – the same woman who truly believed herself liberated!

Rejected Sub-Personalities

We are still dealing with poles opposite to the primary Sub-Personalities; these Sub-Personalities, however, have been rejected, repressed, and hidden in the unconscious, as they do not conform to the preferred values. An individual who has a workaholic Perfectionist in the driver's seat may recognize that some leisure "down time" would be appropriate; on some days, these individuals may well hear their Inner Child whispering in their ear. But there is too much work, the environment is too demanding, the training was too strict – their only option is to grit their teeth and keep moving forward. Later, when retirement arrives, maybe…. or maybe never!

"Demonic" Sub-Personalities

This neologism refers to unintegrated Sub-Personalities connected with basic drives: for example, survival, love, sexuality, hunger. When these polarities are rejected, they can assume a violent, even explosive expression. At these times, they resemble a demon surging up from the depths; they are not, for all that, "demoniacal" in the moral sense of the word. They are only violent because of the way they have been treated. They are attempting by all means to play their vital role in our survival. If nothing comes between them and the primary Sub-Personality that is blocking them, they can break out in a brutal fashion from the dark corner where they were banished. They have a survival drive which is expressed even more violently if the repression was intense.

> Alice is a therapist whose type is Fi/Se (ISFP) Introverted Feeling/Extraverted Sensing. She chose this career since her vocation is to help others; spirituality plays a large role in her life. Her values are humility and service to others. Power struggles are intolerable to her, because harmony must be preserved at all costs – even to

> the point of self-sacrifice.... Until one day when, during a seminar, she turns against the lecturer, accuses him of incompetence, even manipulative behavior, and rushes out of the session in a fit of rage. Her own life force and desire for power, which are perfectly legitimate, but which she has denied for too long, come storming forth in a dramatic fashion, disastrous for all involved.

This can lead to addictions – alcohol, tobacco, or others – in a questionable attempt to fill a void and find a poor solution to a real problem that escapes our conscious awareness. These addictions are accompanied by feelings of guilt and shame that arise in response to the Operating Ego's judgments about this instinctive part that it is unable to regulate, which is something only the Aware Ego would be able to do.

At the societal level, this "outlet" is provided by Mardi Gras style celebrations and carnivals, where for a limited time, the rules are reversed. These periods of "letting go" are even more violent in highly repressive societies.

Mapping of the Unintegrated Ego

The cross of the typological functions enabled us to discover the Operating Ego; in the same way, we can locate the area where its opposite, the Unintegrated Ego, may be located. We will return to our previous examples, adding in the Unintegrated Ego.

Type and Countertype

> Robert, whose type is Introverted Intuiting/Extraverted Thinking, developed a "Primary Self" (another term to identify or "name" the Operating Ego) which functions like an idea factory. The more effective the Primary Self, the more space it takes up, to the point of invading Robert's life.

"The idea factory" / Carpe Diem

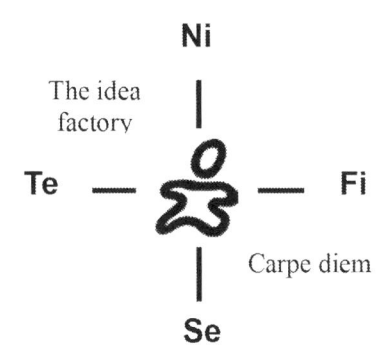

```
                    Ni
         The idea    |
         factory     |
                     ☺
            Te ——   ⚒   —— Fi
                     |
                     |   Carpe diem
                    Se
```

Figure 2.4 – Unintegrated Self, Se/Fi, of Type Ni/Te (Introverted Intuiting/Extraverted Thinking

In doing this, he rejects and banishes into the shadow the opposite pole, which, in the typology is Se/Fi (ESFP) Extraverted Sensing/ Introverted Feeling; this is the opposite of the type or the "countertype". It is characterized by an ease of interaction, an ability to enjoy life's pleasant moments, to be "here and now" rather than in another time and place. It can be summed up in the motto "Carpe diem".

Robert's Operating Ego doesn't think much of this opposite pole. If he were asked to state his opinion (although he probably doesn't even have the time to be interested in the question), he would say that "laziness is a terrible defect, and loafing around killing time never got anyone anywhere. It's a good bet that these sorts of people are all shirkers or scammers".

The Contrast between Introversion and Extraversion

We have seen the "Fighter" within Louise, which has formed around her extraverted functions and leads her boldly onward in her impressive career.

The fighter/The sensitive child

```
                    Ne
                    |      The fighter
          Fi ——— ⊙ ——— Te
                   ℞
        The sensitive child
                    |
                    Si
```

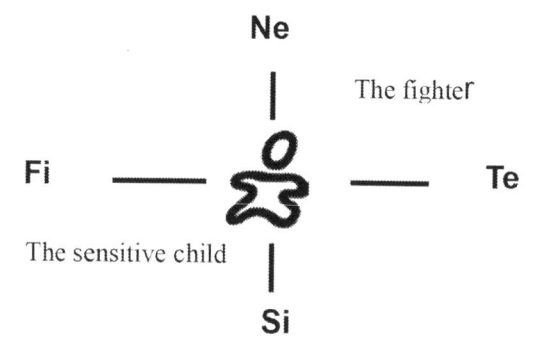

Figure 2.5 – Unintegrated Self Fi/Si of Type Ne/Fi (Extraverted Intuiting/Introverted Feeling)

However, throughout this development, the auxiliary function has been short-circuited, and in doing this, Louise's introverted side has remained in the shadow. She is even less tempted to call on these functions because they are slower, less valued, less brilliant. When she has to face this side of herself, she discovers emotions she isn't used to, and they can be difficult; it is, in any case, a tender area that has remained child-like, and her Primary Self is wary or ashamed of this part. The "Fighter" stifles this voice and condemns it as "hypersensitivity" and "childish whining" when it manifests in others.

The Shadow of the Shadow

Robert's Operating Ego isn't able to stop functioning because every idea conceived must be put into production immediately. It can't ever disengage, even when he is on holiday – in fact the very word exasperates his Operating Ego. Not only is his ability to enjoy the present moment cast into the shadow, but also, to an even greater extent, he is prevented from enjoying the simple pleasures of imagining, daydreaming, and playing, with no obligation to transform these fantasies into reality.

For Robert, individuals of this type, who have Intuiting as the dominant function (as he does) but in the extraverted mode (Ne) "…are just Big Talkers and Know-It-Alls who would be better off saving their breath rather than throwing around ideas that are useless because they don't plan on executing them immediately".

Peter Pan Daydreaming...

Let's dream

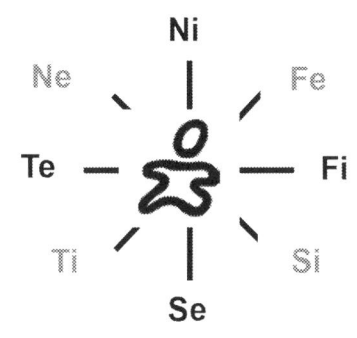

Figure 2.6 – Shadow of the shadow Ne/Ti of Type Ni/Te (Introverted Intuiting/Extraverted Thinking)

In summary

Throughout life, we are required to develop strategies to respond to the challenges of our environment. These strategies make use of our psychic processes in different combinations, resulting in the creation of an Auto-Pilot or Operating Ego which deals effectively with most of the realities of our daily life.

But in doing this, other ways of doing things that might be better adapted to novel situations remain hidden in the shadow. It becomes necessary to exert control over the Auto-Pilot and to be able to unplug it when that might prove useful. This is the goal of the next chapter – Self-Development with Intelligence.

3

SELF-DEVELOPMENT WITH INTELLIGENCE: THE AWARE EGO

NEWS FLASH: The "sclerosis" or psychic fossilization is not inevitable. Two factors lead us in the opposite direction:

- The ability of complex systems to reorganize when the critical threshold of disorganization or inadequacy has been reached; environmental pressures can bring about a modification in our responses. And so at times, a crisis situation transforms an Average Joe into a hero.
- The human aptitude to step back and observe one's actions and modify them accordingly. We are not only "homo sapiens", knowing man, but we are also "sapiens sapiens", man who knows that he knows. Distancing ourselves from something lets us bring in new information which will counteract entropy and system breakdown.

THE THREE LAWS OF CONSCIOUS EVOLUTION

Conscious development occurs according to three laws which are dynamic in nature; they are actions of the psyche, which are, if not always conscious, at least explicit. For this reason, we will use verbs to indicate them:

- Identifying or Naming,
- Disidentifying or Unhooking,
- Integrating and Rebalancing the Opposites.

Identifying or Naming

Until we can name the things that surround us, and the things that happen within us, we have no way of understanding or acting. This is as true in the world of the psyche as it is in all other areas of knowledge; nothing is possible if we cannot perceive, identify, and name what makes us act, both consciously and unconsciously.

It is such a fundamental truth that if we hadn't put this principle into actual practice, we would never have come this far. We would have no way to share and exchange ideas.

In other words, the first step of development consists of identifying how we function and mapping out one's own psyche.

Specifically, this entails:

- Identifying one's psychological type:
    - This can be done in several different ways, and the methods work well in combination rather than using one format exclusively: by readings, such as the ones in the bibliography, or by means of a questionnaire like the one we have developed (the CCTI, see Chapter 7).
    - This may require some time, because there are numerous intervening factors, and discovering one's type requires an effort of clarification.
- Discovering one's favorite strategies and the Sub-Personalities that are at work; recognizing the Operating Ego in its different manifestations and the many different disguises it readily adopts.
- Drawing out a map of the psyche using the function cross, as shown earlier.

This first phase is essential in helping identify what we are talking about. It is not sufficient in and of itself, but this step enables us to move on to the next, which will be easier to accomplish with the help of an experienced practitioner.

Disidentifying or "Unhooking"

The difficulty with the Operating Ego is not in what it knows how to do; it does some things very well, and we would never dream of preventing it from pursuing a particular course of action. The difficulty is that it wants to do everything, or even more directly, it puts itself in our place – the Auto-Pilot mistakes itself for us. When we say "I" (for example "I'm like this or I'm like that..., I like this or that.., I don't like this or that...") with force and conviction, it's not us speaking. It is rather that, unknown to us, our Auto-Pilot has moved in and taken control.

At this point, we need to dissociate the "Aware Ego" from the "Operating Ego"; we need to make our manual controls accessible and not always be operating in automatic mode. We need to discover if there really is a pilot in the plane or if, as in *A Space Odyssey 2001* (Clarke/Kubrick[†]), Hal the computer is going to hijack the controls!

Dissociation is undoubtedly the most difficult part of self-development, but it is also the key stage. It can require strong methods and provoke very intense emotions.

Ways to Disidentify or "Unhook"

Dissociation or disidentification occurs through the realization that the Operating Ego is not us. There are different factors that contribute to this awakening of awareness.

Identifying an energy type is one way. Each Operating Ego has a particular energy, which can be observed in tone of voice, expressions, posture, movements....

Here are some examples of the way in which the different functions and associated Sub-Personalities express themselves.

- Extraverted Thinking shows up in abrupt gestures, a decisive tone of voice, sudden movements, and a rapid, impatient speaking rhythm. It is often associated with the normative parent who imposes and affirms ideas in a clear, or even peremptory manner.
- In contrast, Introverted Feeling appears in very restrained movements, often assuming a prayerful demeanor. Its rhythm

appears slow and considered, yet smooth and precise. It is a discreet and compassionate presence, with calming qualities.
- Introverted Thinking keeps its distance, frowning, looking down haughtily, or it seems to be withdrawn into its ivory tower, like Rodin's "Thinker". It can appear cold and distant at first, and somewhat disinterested or disdainful of common, everyday matters.
- In contrast, Extraverted Feeling throws itself into greetings, expresses interest in everyone, has a kind word for all. Its natural generosity often makes it an overprotective parent – even a "helicopter parent" – with its welcoming, inclusive gestures. It loves to hug and hold. It can immediately see what needs doing to help out, even going so far as to take the cleaning cloth right out of your hands if necessary.
- Extraverted Sensing loves contact and touching; hands are of great importance, and it expresses feelings more often by a gift than by words. It is often the "life of the party", cheerful, livening things up with its spontaneity, "joie de vivre", and funny stories.
- In contrast, Introverted Intuiting appears distant and reserved. It seems to perch up high in an eagle's nest, similar to its spirit animal. This gives it "grandeur", dignity, a serious demeanor, and even a sort of austerity.
- Extraverted Intuiting manifests in an explosion of color and movement, enthusiastic encounters, and a bubbling, sparkling fountain of ideas. It is often associated with Tinkerbell, Peter Pan's "bell fairy".
- In contrast, Introverted Sensing appears quite calm, deliberate, methodical, observant, and enigmatic at first. It functions like a photographic film, recording everything it possibly can.

These brief descriptions, not intended as a complete list, enable us to spot the presence of each of the Sub-Personalities.

The specific technique of Voice Dialogue consists in deliberately granting the floor, or giving a voice, to each part of us, and in doing so, making each voice physically move to a different location. This is done, particularly at the beginning, in the presence of an experienced facilitator.

Although the principle may appear simple, putting it into practice is a much more subtle process. We will have a glimpse into this in Chapter 7.

There are numerous other ways to disidentify from our Operating Ego. We can work through dream interpretation, practise active imagination, draw, dance, sculpt the different parts of ourselves, etc..

Feelings Tied to Disidentification

The Operating Ego can experience this crucial time of disidentification as an actual bereavement and mourning period, as a separation, or at the very least, as a loss of prominence, and this can be painful. These feelings are very strongly felt. They match the same intensity as the dissociation that is occurring, and as such, they indicate that the work is taking place. Despite this, they are not always pleasant emotions, which is why it is necessary to proceed with care, treading gently. In order to describe these stages of inner grieving, we can adapt the model developed in a medical context by Dr. Elisabeth Kübler-Ross[9].

1. Denial. Denial of the dissociation can take many forms. The classic form is quitting or stopping the work. "It serves no purpose!"; "I don't have the time!"; "I don't have any money!" We invent any number of excuses which the Operating Ego uses as justification to ward off the danger.

In training seminars where we teach this method to coaches, we can sometimes clearly see this decisive moment when, overtaken by the Operating Ego, a participant is on the verge of quitting, and we wonder anxiously if he or she will come back. It is a key moment, one which has the potential to turn the process on its head, because if the participant stays, a major milestone has been passed – the step of disidentification. This means that the Operating Ego is ready to give up some of its prerogatives and step back in order to let something else emerge. The hardest part is over.

2. Anger. Deeply wounded, the Operating Ego may react violently. It senses the danger of being discarded, or so it feels, and it reacts in a violent manner. Similar manifestations may appear early on in the self-development work.

---

[9] Kübler-Ross, Elisabeth. *On Grief and Grieving: Finding the Meaning of Grief Through the Five Stages of Loss*

Robert, Ni/Te, (INTJ) Introverted Intuiting/Extraverted Thinking – whom we discussed earlier, undertook a personal development project which required him to travel a long distance. In the course of the first encounter, the coach makes an observation about something Robert has just said: "That sounds completely mental". Like a shot Robert is already at the door crying out "I didn't fly 6,000 miles to listen to this bullshit!" The perceptive coach retorts "Maybe you didn't fly 6,000 miles to leave in such a hurry!"

3. Negotiation. This phase is where the Operating Ego tries to "bargain", or find room for compromise.

> One of our clients, representing so many others at this phase, said to us one day: "This is all well and good as an approach – I'll have no problem applying it in my personal life, but at work, there's no way I can do anything different than what I'm doing now."

And it's quite true: the Operating Ego doesn't know how to do things differently – that is even its main characteristic. For this reason, we do not permit the Sub-Personalities to discuss among themselves. Nor are we trying to get them to reach agreement with one another. That would not be any different from what usually happens, where it is always the strongest voice that wins. Change can only come from another viewpoint, the one that can embrace the opposites, having understood the discord between the different parts which expressed their views.

4. Despondency. Sadness often surprises those who experience it because they also have a sense of making progress. So why this vague heartache and gloominess bordering on depression, eyes welling up with tears, all with no apparent cause? It's simply that the many Parts that make up the Operating Ego don't know how to be subtle and can feel rejected once they are no longer granted all the space. For the Operating Ego, retreat – even just by an inch – means death. And if it disappears, how will the individual survive, since the Operating Ego has been 100% the support system up to now. It is lost and worried.

The Auto-Pilot's reaction is completely normal, and it is of the utmost importance to reassure it that it is not being fired or given early retirement. Quite the contrary, it will continue to be very useful; it will most certainly play its part again, but no longer on its own initiative, because now there is a pilot in the plane who will determine its role. The Auto-Pilot is not "the boss" any longer.

5. Acceptance. The previous four phases are necessary before one can arrive at acceptance. Each of the phases can vary in intensity and duration, but it is neither possible nor desirable to skip any of them. They are a part of the process.

Acceptance brings with it a sense of release; things become less dramatic. We regain a sense of humor – and it lets us laugh at ourselves, rather than joke ironically about others, which is a manifestation of the Operating Ego. We can laugh and cry at the same time; there is a sense of space within us, and new possibilities can be seen on the horizon.

Integrating and Rebalancing the Opposites

At this stage, we have created space to gradually integrate the opposite pole. Our goal is not to struggle and develop one pole to the detriment of the other; nor do we want to exercise the opposite pole in some type of psychic "mind building" similar to "body building". Once the Operating Ego has loosened its grip and let go a little, some space opens up for the opposite pole. I can finally put a hand on each shoulder and "embrace the opposites" rather than be pulled every which way on an inner battlefield.

From this time onward, I can no longer project onto others what I deny in myself; I can no longer hold others responsible for what belongs to me. I start by identifying what arises in me before I blame someone else. And even more importantly: I consider those who irritate me as someone doing a good deed, because they point out clearly what I still have to learn. In fact, we should set up an altar or statues of those who bother us: they are the masters to whom we should pay homage.

This is truly a lifelong discipline, a permanent learning curve. No dodging the issue, no mask to hide behind; one question alone to answer: "Right now, who in me is speaking, thinking, judging, taking action?" It makes us dream of a world in which all individuals would assume their share of responsibility and where anathema, excommunication, and fatwah would no longer be practised!

However, that doesn't mean that everything is equal, that there is no good or evil; our capacity for discernment remains, and it is now even more effective since it is no longer tainted with our projections. Discernment is the role of the Aware Ego.

THE AWARE EGO

The Aware Ego's process is a constant search to disidentify from the dominant pole, or "unhook" from it, and create space for everything we usually reject or are unaware of. It makes it possible to accommodate apparently contradictory drives which are in fact complementary, and also to avoid "sclerosis" or psychic fossilization and internal totalitarianism. It is a process of integration, not exclusion.

The Aware Ego Is...

The Aware Ego is active awareness of the different polarities. It comprises both a distancing or a detachment, because it is not associated with any pole, and a level of involvement, because it expresses a principle of taking action. It is the ability to walk down the street and to see oneself, from the window, walking down the street.

It embraces both poles of each pair of opposites, as it is able to appreciate what each one of them can contribute to the whole. It doesn't favor one over the other. It is the regulator of opposing energies within us, since it is in a position to experience all of our different aspects.

It operates in a dialectic fashion, opening a third way, which is the ridge line between the two peaks, rather than the line following the steepest slope. A creative principle can be stated: "If you are stuck in an 'either-or' dilemma, look for the third solution". This is a perfect description of the Aware Ego.

Having integrated the diverse possibilities, the Aware Ego discerns and makes decisions. It may take more time to arrive at a decision, but it will be a better, more confident decision, without any unforeseen consequences, as the risks and potential problems were anticipated and evaluated at the start. This does not prevent certain aspects of a decision from continuing to be painful, but there will be no further surprises. The Aware Ego is able to wait, not in a passive manner, but in a way which maintains the tension between opposing poles.

> As a young, proactive company director, Lawrence – Fi/Ne (INFP) Introverted Feeling/Extraverted Intuiting – has great success. To achieve this, over the years he has developed a very organized Operating Ego, in contrast to his typological preference. He oversees numerous projects, and his order book is totally filled. He loves his wife and his children, and his social life is very fulfilling. Everything appears to be going extremely well, and yet he feels a sadness that he cannot understand.
>
> By letting his Operating Ego express itself, we find that it is actually this voice that doesn't understand and is quite angry: Lawrence is running the risk of falling back into depression, as has happened before. Everything seems to be smiling on Lawrence, so why is there a cloud hanging over his masterpiece?
>
> By giving voice to this vague sadness and feeling of nostalgia, a much quieter, softer, more introverted energy appears. It is not opposed to Lawrence's success, but it reminds him of his values and basic questions and the importance of taking time for himself. This energy is connected to his dominant function, Introverted Feeling, which has been pushed into the background, as it was not very practical in business.
>
> The Aware Ego can then emerge to take its place between these two equally important energies – action and reflective thought – and integrate the disowned one, in this case reflective thought, which was manifesting as sadness caused by Lawrence's hyperactivity.

There are many images used to portray the Aware Ego. It can be seen as:

- The acrobat balanced on the back of two horses galloping around the ring: with a foot on each horse and the reins in hand, the rider regulates the speed of each horse so that one doesn't take the lead, consistently compensating for the unsteadiness of the horses' movements;

- The corpus callosum which enables communication between the two lobes of the brain;
- The tightrope walker, the symphony conductor, the airplane pilot, the director of a theatrical production, the juggler....

The Aware Ego Is Not...

The Aware Ego isn't anything – it is a constant becoming, a process. As soon as we make it a state of being, the opposite pole arises. The Aware Ego is an unceasing quest, not a finish line. It fulfils a function, but for all that, it is not a fixed entity. It evolves constantly. In fact, the idea of the Aware Ego is more a questioning than a reality. In and of itself, the Aware Ego cannot exist because if it existed, it would create its opposite, and a new Aware Ego would be born from the new opposites. The Aware Ego points the way toward development; it is not a structure in the psyche.

It is not a judge; it does not pass sentence – it is able to see our projections as it does not identify with either side of a duality. It is able to see what we are projecting onto the other. It does not function in a dualistic manner, according to the logic of the "excluded middle". It isn't "either... or..." but rather "both...and...". It reframes situations to help get us out of our limited options.

Conciliation of Opposites

The Aware Ego facilitates the conciliation of opposing poles – not by applying a mathematical averaging operation, but by maintaining the tension between the two opposite poles in order to enable the emergence of new ways of being and acting. Let us look at the example of Maria and observe the four stages of her development.

Maria's type is Fe/Si (ESFJ), so she has Extraverted Feeling as the dominant function and Introverted Sensing as the auxiliary.

Maria has always valued her own warmth, her helpful nature, and her emotional availability. It's why she is loved by all, in both her personal and professional life. She is very strongly identified with this self-image which, however, has brought her to the end of her rope. This is the negative side of Extraverted Feeling associated with Sensing, which easily takes on responsibility. But it is just so natural for her to act in this manner, and everyone is so happy to take advantage of the situation!

On the other hand, she sees the opposite poles Ti/Ne (INTP) Introverted Thinking/Extraverted Intuiting as negative. She considers individuals of this type to be selfish, cold, unsociable, and unreliable. And yet if she could just take a small pinch of this herself, she would be able to grant herself permission to withdraw into herself from time to time. She could re-energize, even if only to be able to continue helping others.

How can Maria's self-development occur in a balanced fashion? As she is both Feeling and Sensing and thus oriented toward practical service to others, this helped her at the start to gain recognition and to find her place in the world. This is what has made her a remarkably efficient daughter, sister, friend, spouse, mother, and human resources consultant. And she is loved by all.

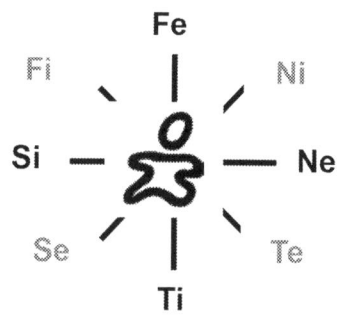

Figure 3.1 – Conciling Opposites for Type Fe/Si (Extraverted Feeling/Introverted Sensing)

Stage One

To avoid this Part doing too much, however, there must first be a conciliation of opposites, the auxiliaries, situated on the horizontal axis. The Aware Ego arises between Introverted Sensing and Extraverted Intuiting, and this brings a sense of lightness, and makes space for spontaneity. Being able to discuss things with others opens new horizons for her, to the point where she quits the consulting firm where she had an important position, in order to set up her own business.

Stage Two

Less tied to her work, she can get some distance and see things differently and thereby involve Introverted Thinking. The other pair of opposites, on the vertical axis this time, will be conciled.

From now on, Maria can sift through social values, choosing the ones she still wishes to uphold, and identifying the ones that have imprisoned her. Her critical sense becomes more acute, and she no longer accepts every personal or professional task that comes her way. People around her notice this change.

Stage Three

By integrating part of the inferior function, Maria gives space to her introverted side, which will reflect back on to her dominant function (Extraverted Feeling), which now finds a more introverted orientation. So Maria can see more clearly which values are her own and recognize that they are just as important as the social values. In practical terms, in her home Maria sets up a very private space which only she can enter.

The resulting profile could be drawn as Fi/Se (ISFP) Introverted Feeling/Extraverted Sensing: the new horizontal axis (diagonally from the bottom left to the top right in Figure 3.1) is that of Extraverted Sensing and Introverted Intuiting, and this opens up a third route towards integration and wholeness.

Stage Four

There remains only the fourth axis (Fi-Te), which will lead Maria to organize her world in accordance with her own values.

In this last phase, we use the future tense, because Maria is not really at this stage yet – and who among us would be? It is difficult enough to work our way through the first two stages; the subsequent stages are even tougher. As with roadmaps, some routes are indicated with a dotted line! And in reality, self-development is, in some ways, much more like walking along a path than driving a highway.

> *In summary*
>
> We are all capable of flying our own plane. Three stages are required to free ourselves from the Auto-Pilot and access the Aware Ego, which has freedom of choice and action: naming the processes at work, disidentifying from the Primary Self, and embracing the opposite poles.
>
> Then we can truly enter into relationships with others. Intelligence of Self leads to Intelligence of the Other, and this is described in the next chapter.

4

THE INTELLIGENCE OF SELF AND OF THE OTHER

THE INTELLIGENCE OF SELF leads us to consider interpersonal relationships not as a simple encounter between two people, but rather as a meeting of two "families", each comprised of preferred and non-preferred processes, dominant and repressed strategies, Auto-Pilot and Shadow.

To fully understand this, two approaches are particularly useful:

- Bringing to light the Bonding Patterns established between the various Sub-Personalities of the individuals present, and
- Clarifying the projections of each individual onto the other by referring to the function dynamics.

BONDING PATTERNS

Unconsciouly everyone tries to reproduce the quality of the very first relationship (usually one's parents) in other relationships, and everyone has two inner aspects: strength and vulnerability. The vulnerability of one person will seek out the strength of the other, and vice versa; however, just as a pendulum can swing in the opposite direction – a typical psychic pattern – this mutual attraction can turn to rejection.

We will therefore look first at a "positive" pattern, in which things are going well for both partners, and then a "negative" pattern, where life is difficult.

To illustrate these patterns, we will take the example of Paul and Valerie.

The "Positive" Bonding Pattern

Paul and Valerie are independent adults, already well along in their careers when they meet in their mid-thirties. Paul is responsible, detailed, methodical, organized, stable, and reserved. In typological terms, he is an Si/Te (ISTJ) Introverted Sensing/ Extraverted Thinking. Valerie is sociable, warm, outgoing, enthusiastic, and generous. In typological terms, she is an Ne/Fi (ENFP) Extraverted Intuiting/ Introverted Feeling. Although their love is not of the thunder and lightning variety, it is a strong enough feeling that they decide to marry. They have kids, buy a new house, and everything goes very well; in the opinion of all concerned, they are an ideal couple, and their families are happy.

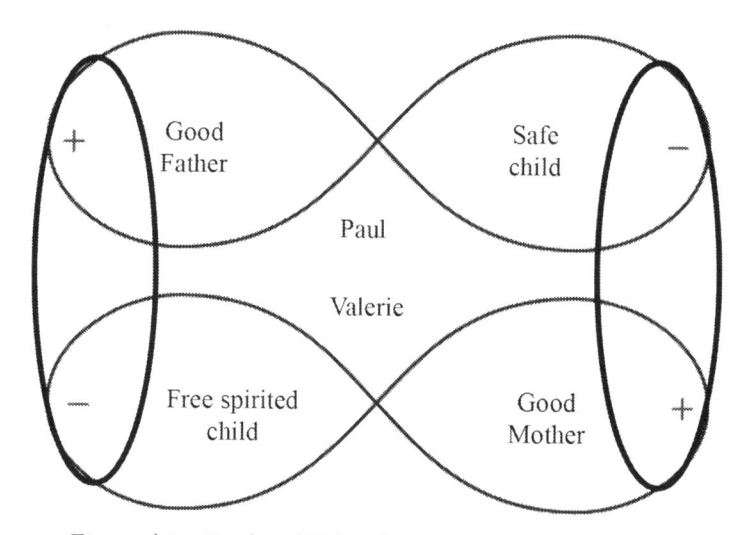

Figure 4.1 – Paul and Valerie's Positive Bonding Pattern

The obvious way in which they complement each other forms the solid cornerstone of their relationship. We can see Paul and Valerie's symmetrical contributions to the relationship, as they each bring a strength to complement the relative vulnerability of the other (in actual fact, the vulnerability was seen as attractive at the start of the relationship).

1. Paul's strength – He is a good father who takes charge of the household.
2. Valerie's vulnerability – She is a free-spirited child.

3. Valerie's strength – She is a good mother, communicative and in touch with the external social world.
4. Paul's vulnerability – He is a lonely little boy who has difficulty communicating.

This pattern is positive in that:

- Both partners are appreciated for what they can contribute to the relationship.
- The relationship is an enjoyable experience, and both partners want it to last.

The "Negative" Bonding Pattern

The positive pattern rarely lasts a long time. Sooner or later, under some form of duress, it will turn into its opposite. This can occur very rapidly and unexpectedly.

There are two different causes for this disruption:

- External conditions can create stress for one of the partners or for both. In this case, most commonly, there will be an exaggeration of the dominant part. In an emergency, the Auto-Pilot intensifies its efforts to meet the demands of the situation. Each partner thus does more of the same thing, as if to find reassurance in the areas where they are most comfortable, but each does too much.
- The relationship breaks down. The positive pattern is pleasant, of course, but in the long run, it can become stifling. One partner manages to disrupt the pattern, which does not necessarily put an end to the relationship.

> For Paul and Valerie, tough times arrive: a job loss, difficulties with the children, the death of a parent which, for both of them, reawakens the pain of earlier losses.
>
> Things just aren't the same any more.

"Paul acts like a dictator", says Valerie. "He's always trying to supervise me; I don't do anything right; he criticizes me; I've got no privacy; he's jealous when I see anyone else but him!"

"Valerie is irresponsible", says Paul. "She has no money sense; she has irrational temper tantrums, and I have to take on everything single-handedly".

Fairly or not, the pendulum swings. Valerie becomes depressed, and Paul feels abandoned and crushed by all his responsibilities.

Paul and Valerie's complementarity has become a source of conflict. Let's look closer at this change of perspective:

1. The good father has become a dictator who monitors everything in the house (strength).
2. The "irresponsible" child is punished (weakness).
3. In return, Valerie withdraws emotionally (strength).
4. Paul is left feeling abandoned (weakness).

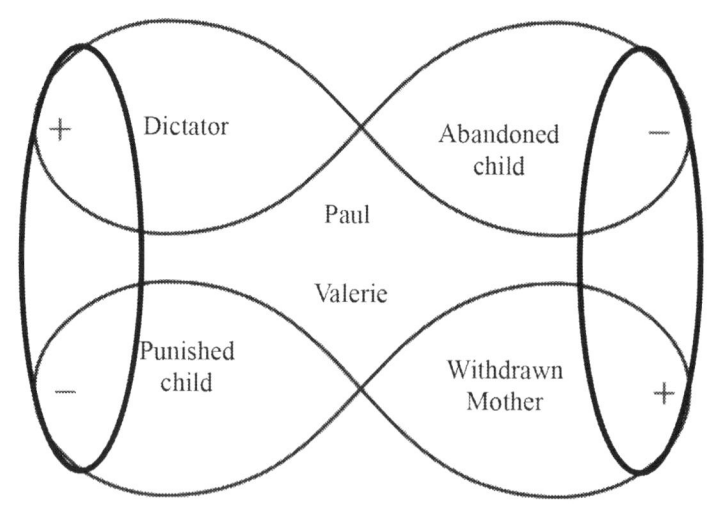

Figure 4.2 – Paul and Valerie's negative Bonding Pattern

This pattern is negative in that:

- Each person can only see the other's power and therefore considers the other an adversary.
- Both partners are unhappy in the relationship, but they do not know how to change it, having rejected their own disowned part and left the burden of it with the other partner (the child for Paul, the adult woman for Valerie).

To change the relationship, they would have to rediscover their Operating Ego, which has taken hold, and from their Aware Ego, they would both have to be able to integrate aspects of the other's Operating Ego into their own Aware Ego Process. Without this occurring, we end up in a situation similar to the two rowers, each one leaning far out over the side of the rowboat.

The person on the left will say that he really must lean so far left in order to balance the rowboat, because the person on the right is destabilizing the boat.... and vice versa. Of course, it would be much easier for both just to sit quietly in the middle. Even if they can agree to do that, they will have to coordinate their movements to succeed, or one will have to start and the other make adjustments, otherwise the rowboat will capsize.

Observations

- There is no avoiding Bonding Patterns; our Sub-Personalities most certainly do exist, and they do play a role.
- To be considered a Bonding Pattern, the relationship must have existed for a certain length of time. A brief encounter does not automatically give rise to a bonding pattern, and we cannot necessarily analyze it in detail. Nor does it involve the reversal into its opposite
- Positive patterns are not better than negative ones; although we might feel infinitely better at these times, we might also feel bored or half asleep!

- Maintaining a positive pattern whatever the cost ("We have never argued") can bring about a "sclerosis" or fossilization of the relationship, because in order to keep the peace, we might:
  - hold back from saying or doing something we feel like saying or doing, for fear of upsetting the other person, or
  - feel obligated to say or do something we don't feel like saying or doing, in order to please the other.
- It is possible for a relationship to progress without constantly swinging wildly from a positive Bonding Pattern to a negative Bonding Pattern. This requires that both partners first succeed in disidentifying from their Auto-Pilot.
- In this respect, a long-term relationship (personal or professional) which is valued by both partners can prove to be a good way to grow and develop, because each partner reflects what the other is missing.
- When the same type of Bonding Pattern repeats itself regularly with different people, it is high time to look carefully at the problem. There is very certainly a projection occurring, and clarifying it will enable us to avoid the same pitfalls in the future. This is often the case when we move on to a new partner; sooner or later, the same type of problem arises.

PROJECTIONS AND JUDGMENTS

Defining Terms

What is a Projection?

A projection is a psychic mechanism by which we attribute to another person thoughts and emotions which belong to us. These are either negative aspects that we do not want to see in ourselves, or they are positive aspects that we cannot acknowledge in ourselves. "Why are you sulking?" says the grumpy spouse to the other, who hasn't yet said a word.

To speak of projection, there must be a strong emotional component attached to the judgment or attitude. It is possible to like or dislike something or someone, but there is probably a projection involved if the preference or aversion is expressed in terms such as: "She is absolutely wonderful – I've never met anyone so perfect", or "I hate him", "I can't stand him", "He's the worst____I've ever seen", "He drives me crazy". These words are spoken forcefully, abruptly, in an absolute, generalizing manner, and leave no place for doubt or correction.

Projection can be positive or negative.

Positive Projections

We admire the other for a quality that we don't have, or that we think we don't have. In fact, we have all the potential, but some qualities are so far removed from us, completely opposite to our Auto-Pilot, that we cannot see them in ourselves. Incidentally, we generally ascribe more positive qualities to the other than are truly present – but why be miserly! – when we are filled with admiration, we do not scrimp on compliments. "The grass is always greener on the other side of the fence", or so goes the saying.

Being able to recognize in another person a quality that we think we don't have is, however, clearly a sign that the quality already exists within us: "You would not seek me if you had not found me"[10].

> Thus Fran, a very sociable Englishwoman, upon meeting an Italian woman, exclaims: "It's such an expressive language – I love Italian", while she is actually very expressive herself, in her own culture.

Negative Projections

The other person bothers us precisely because of this difference, which becomes a source of argument. We can only see the bad sides now, and not the ones which evoked the positive projection. Where is the justification for this turnaround? It may be the passing of time, a current stressor, or the discovery that the other is not as perfect as the image we had created. Disillusionment follows, and without an awakening of awareness, there will be a breakdown of the relationship.

---

[10] PASCAL†, *Pensées*, VII, 553.

Judgments

Judgments are very similar to projections: they are a type of projection in the form of an accusation or condemnation of the other. We move from "I hate him" to "He is detestable". Judgments are often expressed as generalizations: "All Cretans are liars" (Epimenides[†]); "All ____ are untrustworthy, lazy, etc.". As with projections, judgments arise in our Auto-Pilot because it views the opposite pole in an extremely negative way.

The typological approach enables us to focus on the areas where projections can easily occur, although we make no claim whatsoever that we can fully capture the infinite diversity of possible situations.

Projection from Inferior to Dominant

I have an inferior function that is my coworker's dominant function.
There are two possibilities:

- Either I admire what he can do, while I do it very badly or not at all,
- Or it bothers me, and since I see his dominant function through the lens of my inferior function, I come to the conclusion that it is terribly inept and inappropriate.

In this way, Robert (Ni/Te) Introverted Intuiting/Extraverted Thinking, whose seriousness, intellectual rigor, and even austerity were described earlier, has a friend, Gerard, who is in all things his exact opposite. Fun-loving, "bon vivant", pragmatic, willing to engage with others, resourceful, not in the least bit interested in theorizing. In typological terms, he is an Se/Fi (ESFP) Extraverted Sensing/Introverted Feeling.

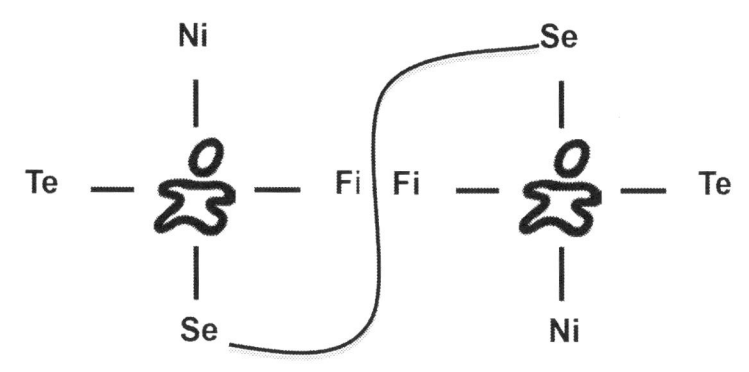

Becoming Who You Are with the Intelligence of Self

Figure 4.3 – Projections Ni/Te-Se/Fi Introverted
Intuiting/ Extraverted Thinking and
Extraverted Sensing/Introverted Feeling

Robert's inferior function is Extraverted Sensing, which is Gerard's dominant, and vice versa, which can lead to two different situations:

- **Positive projection** – Robert unabashedly admires Gerard's ability to adapt and his sociability. He finds him so fascinating that he brings Gerard into his circle of friends and associates to become "one of them", and he imitates his ways of doing things. And it often happens that the projection goes both ways: Gerard may also be fascinated by Robert's intellect, his ability to synthesize and forecast. He takes every possible opportunity to consult Robert, and admires the opinions and advice Robert offers.
- **Negative projection** – Robert considers Gerard to be an "I-don't-give-a-damn" slacker, always ready to talk, but never taking action when necessary, spinning in the breeze like a weathervane. Every time Gerard shows up late, grinning (and this happens often), Robert is on the verge of an angry outburst. As for Gerard, he is exasperated by the arrogance of "Mr. Know-It-All" and his tendency to stick to Gerard like a leech "because he can't even damn well take a break from his agenda to appreciate the people he works with and have a bit of fun".

Projection from Dominant to Opposite Dominant

Projection Mechanism

I have the same dominant function as my coworker. But whereas mine is introverted, my coworker's is extraverted (or the reverse). It appears that in this case, a negative projection is more common than a positive projection – this is an observation based on experience that is not supported by scientific data! Why might there be a projection? Because each individual believes that the other has the "right" function, but is using it "incorrectly" since it is used differently. It's not just a wrong note (after all, anyone can hit a wrong note) but it's the wrong key, as if the instrument were out of tune – and that is constant torture.

As an example, we will look at the case of two department heads in the same company, both apparently achieving great success.

Frederick is a Ti/Se (ISTP), whose dominant function is Introverted Thinking and whose auxiliary function is Extraverted Sensing. He's a man of practical action – a perfect example of professional competency. The strategy that he pursues within his department is patently clear to him; he expects it to be equally clear for his team, as actions speak for themselves. If something is unclear, he will respond to any questions for clarification.

Louis is a Te/Ni (ENTJ), whose dominant function is Extraverted Thinking and whose auxiliary function is Introverted Intuiting. He presents the overall scope, describing what he wants in a clear and occasionally curt manner. If things aren't clear, it's because someone wasn't listening.

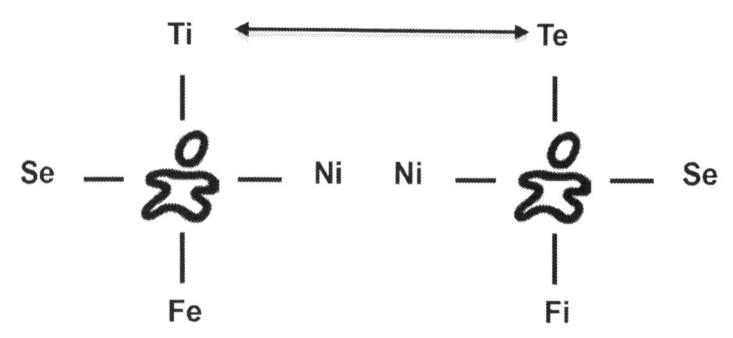

Figure 4.4 – Projection Ti/Se-Te/Ni: Introverted Thinking/ Extraverted Sensing and Extraverted Thinking/Introverted Intuiting

Frederick finds Louis to be very abrupt in his manner: "he's so forceful"; he charges straight into things without thinking and behaves like a bull in a china shop. Making quick decisions is of no value whatsoever if it means you run "head-on into a wall".

Louis finds Frederick's slow decision-making to be utterly exasperating. "He's such a nit-picker!" Louis believes that a bad decision made quickly is better than a good one made too late.

Examples

In the tables which follow, we give examples of positive and negative projections:

- Projection by an inferior (or tertiary) function in relation to the opposite function – dominant (or auxiliary); for example, by Extraverted Sensing as an inferior function in relation to Introverted Intuiting as dominant.
- Projection by a function in any position in relation to the same function in the opposite position; for example, by Introverted Sensing in relation to Extraverted Sensing.

We emphasize that these examples are grounded in our experience; they are not in any way an attempt to provide a systematic description.

Table 4.1 – Projections by One Function onto the Opposite Function

Function	Projection by One Function onto the Opposite Function	
	Positive	**Negative**
Extraverted Sensing onto Introverted Intuiting	"Ah, if only I had that ability to foresee things; I would follow someone with such forward-looking vision to hell and back!"	"These abstract thinkers lost in thought drive me absolutely crazy. They have their head stuck in the clouds, and they aren't grounded in reality."
Introverted Sensing onto Extraverted Intuiting	"I'm awestruck by such creative talent; I feel like a miserable beggar in comparison!"	"It's easy to talk. But it's always the same people who have to pick up the pieces afterward."
Extraverted Intuiting onto Introverted Sensing	"How lucky they are to have their feet so firmly planted on the ground and find everything they need so quickly!"	"I hate these crazy, narrow-minded obsessive bureaucrats. They stop me from really living life to the fullest."
Introverted Intuiting onto Extraverted Sensing	"I really admire their easy style and manner; it looks like everything just flows effortlessly for them – never any headaches!"	"It's a nice life when you can enjoy all the glory at the expense of others. No sense of responsibility – it's so exasperating."
Extraverted Thinking onto Introverted Feeling	"When I'm around him, I feel like a bull in a china shop: if only I had that subtle touch!"	"'Weighing fly eggs in spider web scales…'(Voltaire †) This is obviously not someone who cares much about efficiency."
Introverted Thinking onto Extraverted Feeling	"What social grace! What ability to unify people! I feel like a total wallflower."	"Run away, save yourself, the missionaries are coming, and we will be converted by force!"
Extraverted Feeling onto Introverted Thinking	"I stand in awe of these people who don't have to champion every little cause. I wouldn't have to be the "universal mother."	"Nit-picking when there is so much suffering all around – you really have to have a rock in place of your heart…."
Introverted Feeling onto Extraverted Thinking	"What clarity of mind! What ability to stand his ground and speak his mind, instead of being trampled."	"When it comes to cutting to the core of a question, he is very good; the downside is that if you're always cutting to the core, you pretty much kill everything."

Table 4.2 – Projections by One Function onto the Same Function in the Opposite Orientation

Function	Projection by One Function onto the Same Function in the Opposite Orientation	
	Positive	**Negative**
Extraverted Sensing onto Introverted Sensing	"Ah – if only I were as well organized, that would make me even more effective, and I would have even more time to enjoy life."	"These detail-obsessed, know-it-all maniacs! All they do is get in the way!"
Introverted Sensing onto Extraverted Sensing	"If only I could slow down and smell the roses – make the most of my time instead of always trying to do better!"	"It really bothers me to see him wasting his talent puttering away at any little project, just reinventing the wheel!"
Extraverted Intuiting onto Introverted Intuiting	"I could avoid saying some pretty idiotic things if I followed that example and spoke only after really thinking things through!"	"It's easy to look intelligent 24 hours after everyone else has gone to the effort of expressing their thoughts."
Introverted Intuiting onto Extraverted Intuiting	"How great it would be to be able to speak so freely; I feel like I'm completely tongue-tied when I hear him speaking."	"It bugs me the way these Know-it-Alls throw ideas around; any idiot can have ideas, but you have to do something with them!"
Extraverted Thinking onto Introverted Thinking	"I'd really like to have that level-headedness and that remarkable capacity to let a decision 'ripen' in its own time instead of rushing through things to get them off my desk as soon as possible."	"It's good to think things over, but splitting hairs lengthwise – that's bad! You need to be able to be decisive and take action without constant quibbling over details!"
Introverted Thinking onto Extraverted Thinking	"What a dream to be able to act so decisively, no hesitating! I would avoid going around in circles and getting in my own way."	"I can't stand people who don't make a distinction between decision-making and thinking. They might as well just get a chainsaw to decide the issues – cut, slash, done!"
Extraverted Feeling onto Introverted Feeling	"How does he do it – he appears to influence others by his presence alone. I feel like I always miss the mark."	"It's all well and good to hold nice values and to worry about the meaning of life, but couldn't you maybe just spend a little time taking care of others too?"
Introverted Feeling onto Extraverted Feeling	"I admire his conviction, and capacity to have others share the same values. I feel useless, compared to such generosity."	"It bugs me to see him constantly preaching the good word; it's too much. Have a little decency, please!"

> *In summary*
>
> The meeting of two people is, in fact, the meeting of two "families": the interactions or Bonding Patterns that can then play out are varied and numerous. If they are not clarified, they can give rise to projections and judgments which put the relationship at risk.
>
> This is one further reason to examine the practical ways we can apply Intelligence of Self. That is the goal of Part II.

PART II

PUTTING THE INTELLIGENCE OF SELF INTO PRACTICE

HAVING MAPPED OUT THE GREAT LAWS governing the development of awareness, let us now turn to the ways in which they can materialize for each of us. We will consider four areas:

1. How can Intelligence of Self offer new solutions in certain situations?
2. What kind of help can we ask for to travel this path more easily? What does a coach do?
3. Which methods should be used?
4. How can the methods be used by an individual to practise "self-coaching"?

5

SOME TYPICAL SITUATIONS

INTELLIGENCE OF SELF is a way of life, a constant quest throughout life, a permanent questioning: "Who in me is speaking?" This question is at times, crucial; it becomes "the" burning question. We have identified some of these key moments, either because they have great importance in our lives, or because they frequently give rise to questions. Let us be perfectly clear that these are some typical examples, and not an exhaustive overview. We will look at:

- Three situations arising in one's personal life:
    - childhood and formation of the psyche;
    - intimate relationships, perfect examples of Bonding Patterns;
    - the aging process;
- Three situations arising in one's professional life:
    - choice of career and career progression;
    - the managerial role;
    - the Aware Ego and politics.

CHILDHOOD

The children that we once were, the children that we have or will perhaps have, the children in our lives, and our own Inner Child interest us first and foremost. In point of fact, when we ask, respondents often say first that it is their children that matter most to them.

So let us discuss some of the questions that these different children raise.

Pierre Cauvin – Geneviève Cailloux

At What Age Can We Identify a Child's Psychological Type?

Even if psychic functions reveal themselves through behaviors, they cannot be reduced to them. In fact, only the person concerned can really determine his mode of operation. This is by definition impossible with very young children, because even if they were aware of their type, they would, in any event, lack the vocabulary to talk about it.

The observer, parent, or educator is thus reduced to making careful hypotheses based on what the child does or says. The goal of these hypotheses is not to "discover" the child's type, but rather to understand him, to put ourselves in the child's shoes, and to avoid prejudices. We are not necessarily focused on the type as a whole, but on certain of its most obvious characteristics.

The orientation of the dominant function, extraverted or introverted, appears very early on. One has only to observe the baby's movements and its gaze as it lies in the cradle: some children are focused deeply within for long periods at a time, and wait for a stimulus in order to react, and others are cooing, moving, attracting attention, and reacting to everything around them.

The dominant function itself, or some of its characteristics, may manifest as early as 5 or 6 years of age, sometimes sooner. Nicknames given to the child are often suggestive of this function. During a seminar, three young women, all Te/Ni (ENTJ), were asked their childhood nicknames. As we know that the dominant function, Extraverted Thinking, has a propensity to rule over its surroundings, no one will be surprised to learn that their nicknames were: "captain", "commander", or "general".

> Stella, 8 years old, has no inhibitions about being the leader of her brothers, sister, and cousins. Her grandfather says to her with a smile "Well aren't you a real little general!" And, with a hearty laugh, she replies: "Of course I am!" There is no judgment in this exchange, no approval or disapproval – simply the recognition of her personality.
>
> Similarly, this comment made by Melanie, another 8-year-old, is very typical of her type, "NT" (Intuiting/Thinking): "I've learned something important: once you know how to read, you will never be bored again."

In practical terms, awareness of oneself can begin at an early age. Interested children can have a clear idea of their psychological type as early as 10-12 years of age, provided that a vocabulary adapted to the age group is used.

Educating the Aware Ego

In the context of Intelligence of Self, the ultimate goal of our education is not achieving any one objective in particular – finding a career, being happy, succeeding in life.... The goal is enabling our children or pupils to develop the ability to "embrace the opposites", to exercise the faculty of discernment, or in short, to develop the "Aware Ego".

This requires the following attitudes.

Take the Child Seriously

Initially the goal is not to achieve a specific behavior, even if that may also be necessary. Educating the Aware Ego is not like training a circus animal to jump through hoops to please its trainer. It essentially aims at helping the child to see his varying attitudes clearly, to understand his different motivations, to accept his ambivalence, and to let his different parts express themselves.

What happens within is every bit as important as what happens in the outer world, if not more so. A classic example is the recurring dream in which a monster chases the sleeping child. It is useless to turn on the light and look under the bed to prove that there is no lion hiding under it. No one believes there is a lion under the child's bed, but there well and truly is a lion in his head, a real lion of the psyche. So rather than illustrating the absurd – the non-existence of something that doesn't exist! – it would be better to speak to the child about what really exists: the lion seen in the nightmare. We can ask him to draw it, to think about what in his life might resemble this lion, or even follow the steps described in the section "By the Light of our Dreams" found in Chapter 7.

Respect the Child's Type

Knowing the child's psychological type enables us to better understand how the child functions and to respect his growth. In other words, we let the child develop the adaptation strategies which best correspond to his preferred psychic functions.

This is extremely difficult to do, because many parents, with the best intentions in the world, tend to want for their children the same things that worked for them: "It's for your own good!"; "You'll thank me for this one day!" There are countless examples of "counter-type" development; we encounter them every day working with our clients.

> Emma, an introverted type, lives in a family where extraversion is the norm. From very early on she is virtually persecuted: "Don't just stay alone in your room all day!", "Don't you have anything better to do than just sit there reading by yourself?", "You're not very sociable, are you?", and so on.... This happens to such a degree that she feels guilty stealing time away to be alone, and she spends an inordinate amount of energy trying to do more of what is expected of her. Noah, who has Introverted Feeling as dominant function, likes to please others in a concrete way (his auxiliary function is Extraverted Sensation). He is interested in psychology, but since he is – unfortunately! – good at math, family and school pressures steer him toward engineering. As he is motivated even more strongly to please others, he undertakes this program of studies, even succeeding brilliantly. But he never truly feels like he fits in. So he attempts to get out of the technical world as quickly as possible, in order to become involved in the field of human resources, where at first, his lack of training is a quite a handicap.

Play with the Opposites

Respecting the development of the child's psychological type doesn't prevent us from helping him become aware of the opposite polarities. In fact, a psychological type includes the complete range of all possibilities. If it is appropriate not to go against spontaneous preferences, especially at the beginning, it is just as necessary to show that there are other ways of doing things, and these ways might be more useful in some circumstances.

> Oliver, whose dominant function is Extraverted Intuiting (Ne), who really enjoys jumping from one idea to the next. He takes pleasure in discovery, not in deep investigation. However, he finds it necessary to keep his notebook more or less up to date, otherwise the bad grades start to accumulate.

Adolescence is an important moment when it comes to this experimentation with opposites. In type development, at around this age, the auxiliary function begins to develop. And so, as we saw earlier, there is a change in the function's nature (from a Perceiving function to a Judging function or vice versa) and a change in its orientation (from extraversion to introversion, or vice versa).

> So Jacob, whose dominant function is introverted, spends most of his childhood on his own, avoiding group activities as much as he possibly can. He would have loved to be homeschooled. However, in adolescence, he starts to take part in an amateur theater club and take on a variety of related responsibilities. When he is 15, even decides to go camping with a group of friends.

Developing the Parental Aware Ego

In order for parents to accomplish the preceding tasks, it is first necessary to disidentify from their own Auto-Pilot, or run the risk of transmitting it to the child. Developing one's own Aware Ego is without a doubt the principal task for a parent, and the most significant support a parent can give to a child.

In accordance with the inescapable law of "what goes around, comes around" – much like a boomerang – everything that we do not wish to acknowledge in ourselves comes back sooner or later in one form or another. If it doesn't occur in our life directly, then it will occur through our children's lives. They are particularly good at acting out what we have repressed. This is so true that it has become a favorite topic for cartoonists and caricaturists.

The children of the 1960's "Flower children" became the social-status-seeking "Yuppies", and psychedelic flower power T-shirts gave way to three-piece suits.

The Mystery of Childhood

> She was 10 months old; she had awoken in the middle of the night. I took her in my arms, and she looked at me; two dark eyes which revealed an inner life that I hadn't suspected before this moment. I looked back at her in turn. We stayed like this for a long moment. A real meeting. And I continued holding her for a long time after she fell back to sleep, with a soft, rhythmic breathing, almost a purring.

From birth, a complete person is present, holding within all the seeds of his future development. James Hillman[†] has devoted a number of beautiful texts to describing the uniqueness of each human being, which is evident from early infancy and particularly visible during childhood; this singularity cannot be reduced to any psychologizing or mechanistic model. According to his theory, each of us carries within a unique image, which is our essence, and which expresses our vocation.

This is to say that beyond all explanation, there remains the mystery of each person, of individuality, of originality. "The call to an individual destiny is not an issue between faithless science and unscientific faith. Individuality remains an issue for psychology – a psychology that holds in mind its prefix, "psyche", and its premise, soul…."[11]

Each one of us is thus the bearer of a unique project, a seed that is with us at birth and which unfolds throughout the course of our life. Depending on our preferences or background, we may call this a soul, a "daimon", our Inner Child, the primitive engram, our calling…. It is the essence of our life, giving it flavor. It gives our life its meaning, which we discover gradually by exploring the paths which open before us. The entire course of our life is a progressive actualization, in greater or lesser detail, of all we were given at birth.

---

[11] Hillman, James. *The Soul's Code; In Search of Character and Calling.* Random House, 1996, page 11.

It is also the inner space of our deepest part, the one showing the path toward intimacy and love. The romantic encounter is with the person who will crystalize our destiny, giving it at once its universality and its singularity. How this encounter occurs, how it evolves over time, in step with each individual partner's growth, is the topic of the next section.

INTIMATE RELATIONSHIPS (COUPLES)

Forming the basis of all human societies, the couple is one of the most important settings for relationships to form and emotional patterns to play out. This is even more evident in contemporary Western society, where a couple's partnership is founded on love as well, and is thus infused with high expectations. So life within a couple becomes a shared journey and, from the time it becomes a long-term commitment, it is a shared pathway toward the Aware Ego of each of the partners. It seems to us that in this respect, life within a couple can be a particularly lofty and demanding spiritual path.

To better understand what this route consists of, we will examine:

- The cycle of Bonding Patterns, and
- The basis of this type of relationship and the ways it can be jeopardized.

Bonding Patterns in Intimate Relationships (Couples)

To guide us, we will follow the story of Louis and Brigitte, a couple who experience highs and lows, going from blessed to cursed!

Positive Bonding Pattern

> Louis was born into a family that was well known in the area. Having completed his law degree, he met Brigitte, who had just finished a diploma in secretarial studies. Brigitte came from very modest circumstances. Deeply in love with one another, they

married despite their families' reluctance. They soon had three children. Louis worked in a large company; Brigitte devoted herself to the children's care and upbringing

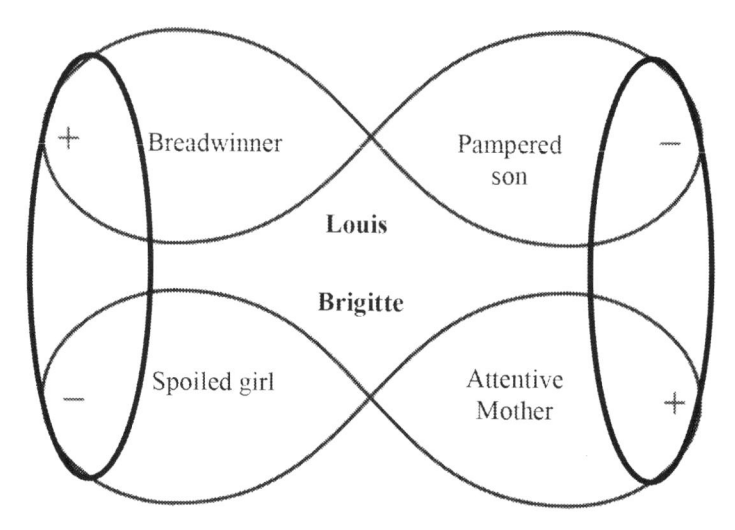

Figure 5.1 – Positive Bonding Pattern of Couple – Louis and Brigitte

A positive pattern is established:

1. Louis is the breadwinner. His type (Si/Te, ISTJ) Introverted Sensing/Extraverted Thinking, predisposes him to adopt a traditional role in the family; he considers himself the head.
2. Brigitte is willing to step back into a supporting role for everything related to the external world, particularly financial issues. In fact, Louis takes charge of both their capital and their income.
3. But within the household, Brigitte takes care of everything. Moreover, she believes that this is her wifely duty, and the Patriarch, governing the woman's traditional role, rejoices to find her such a docile subject!
4. This suits Louis entirely, as he finds himself in the position of the pampered child.

This is a well-established, typical, even classic scenario that we encounter in a variety of forms in countless households. Societal evolution has made it less common at the beginning of a relationship than it was several decades ago. The division of roles is less clear-cut, and women often take on an active role in the external world, at times even more important than their spouses. But strangely, when a child is born, the Patriarch shows up with great fanfare, and for a short period of time, even the most liberated couples often return, almost inevitably, to the pattern described above.

> Louis and Brigitte's positive pattern lasts until a combination of events occurs to change it:
>
> - The children grow up, and Brigitte's presence is less necessary.
> - With time on her hands, she can work on her lifelong dream, and she returns to her studies, obtaining her degree in counseling psychology.
> - Louis loses his job and opens his own consulting business.
> - Louis and Brigitte consider this the perfect opportunity to work together.
>
> At first, Louis and Brigitte are able to maintain the essence of the positive pattern, which is familiar and comfortable. In other words, Louis remains the boss, and Brigitte does the secretarial work; her name doesn't even appear on the company title. But very soon, this situation becomes untenable, and a negative pattern develops; this is all the more noticeable as the company is having difficulties starting out. Times are tough.

Negative Bonding Pattern

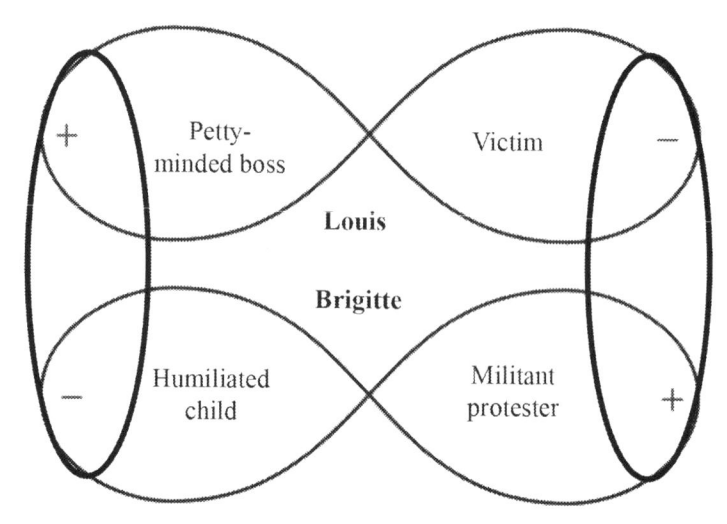

Figure 5.2 – Negative Bonding Pattern of Couple – Louis and Brigitte

1. Louis is no longer the breadwinner he was previously. The administrative and financial authority he retains is quickly seen by Brigitte to be somewhat arbitrary.
2. Facing the "petty-minded boss", Brigitte feels oppressed; she falls back into a posture of humiliated child, which she hates.
3. She reacts by adamantly asserting her place in the company – her own workspace, the right to be consulted in management decisions. The militant protester claims her place at center stage.
4. Louis, in response, becomes a victim whose competency is no longer acknowledged. He feels belittled.

It is a cacophonous dialogue of the deaf – no one is talking at all at this stage. We can easily imagine the exchanges between the petty-minded boss and the activist. As for the victim and the humiliated child, they each retire to their separate corners, both expressing their suffering in a different way. Brigitte cries, which exasperates Louis, and he withdraws into his ivory tower, which makes Brigitte even more unhappy.

And of course, their respective Auto-Pilots do everything they can to solve the problem, which only complicates things, because these actions are no longer adapted to the situation:

- Louis' Auto-Pilot longs to regain its role as the strong man whose authority stems from being the one who provides for his family – but how can it do this when there is no money coming in?
- Brigitte's Auto-Pilot tries to keep her in the role of the submissive wife – but another part of her has ideas and a desire to see them come to life.

Fortunately, Louis and Brigitte love one another and are willing to work things out. They will both gradually disidentify from their Auto-Pilot in order to make space for their Aware Ego, and they will be able to integrate a new role without necessarily disowning or rejecting what is still very useful from a past role. In practical terms:

- Brigitte becomes particularly aware that she has been required to develop the behaviors of a supportive parent, something which doesn't correspond well to her psychological type (Fi/Ne – INFP). In fact, she has called on an organizing, planning energy that is not easy for her to access.
- Getting some distance from her Operating Ego, she is able to integrate her need to take her rightful place in the assertive manner characteristic of her inferior function, Extraverted Thinking, but without being aggressive.
- Louis, in his own right, carries out a review of his system. In theory, actually, he is quite prepared to see his wife assume a greater role in the company and to see her as his associate, no longer just his secretary; however, the practical application of this idea bumps up against the customary habits that he has followed up to now. He is therefore required to make a number of changes; for example, transferring the partnership in legal and marketing terms so that "his" company truly becomes "their" company.

The Aware Ego in Intimate Relationships (Couples)

From this point forth, Louis and Brigitte will be able to speak to each other from their Aware Egos, at least some of the time. This doesn't guarantee that company revenues will go through the roof or that life will always be a bed of roses, but it does mean that they will be able to understand one another, make better informed decisions, and in short, really feel like they are full and equal "partners".

Some Key Elements

If this dialogue between Aware Egos is our goal, how do we get there? There are a few key elements which are worth emphasizing.

Inevitability of the Cycles

The alternation between positive and negative Bonding Patterns is a fact of the human condition. It is neither good or bad. It just is. Similarly, there cannot be more relational stability between two Aware Egos than there is stability of an individual Aware Ego. All roads have their peaks and valleys. Being two in a relationship often emphasizes the swings, making judgments and projections more intense and more obvious; this can be painful, and it is also a wonderful opportunity to make progress, provided that we are not too quick to throw in the towel. Proclaiming that we have been disappointed by the other partner and charging right into a new relationship, like a Don Juan or a Bluebeard, puts us at very high risk for an infinite repetition of the same process – simply with different partners who are, nonetheless, quite similar.

Intimacy and Vulnerability

In a Bonding Pattern, each partner occupies a high and a low position or the role of parent to the other's child and vice versa (the role of child to the other's parent); these positions are symmetrical in relationship one to the other.

What distinguishes a positive from a negative Bonding Pattern is the perception each partner has of the relative strength of these positions:

- In the positive Bonding Pattern, both partners are sensitive to the vulnerability of the other and wish to contribute something. Both are also aware of their own fragility and find strength in the other partner.
- In the negative Bonding Pattern, both partners perceive the other as a threat and can only see the other's strength that must be countered. This leads to an escalation of violence.

Under these conditions, the situation can only harden and become stuck, and both partners attempt to protect themselves from the other. In order for the relationship to be fulfilling and alive, it becomes necessary to share their vulnerability in a trusting environment. This is certainly more easily said than done, and to get to this stage, they must create the necessary conditions.

A Time for Sharing

The Aware Ego cannot emerge if we do not create opportunities for this; vulnerability can't be shared in the middle of a crisis – it would be like sending an unprotected child out among armed gangsters!

Life most certainly offers moments for warm, caring and sharing. But the pressures of day-to-day life are such that these moments can be few and far between. To ensure an orderly life as a couple, it becomes important to plan for two types of meetings:

- Meetings of a semi-technical nature to manage administrative and financial aspects in the couple's (or family's) life. These meetings should be well enough organized and last long enough that the Aware Ego of each participant can emerge, rather than the Auto-Pilot; the latter has too great a tendency to decide to do things its own way without consideration for the opposite point of view – which is often held by the other partner.

- Personal encounters during which both partners can speak about themselves, their experiences, emotions, and dreams – in short, about everything that constitutes the richness of their inner life.

The "Captivating Third"

A relationship as a couple does not prohibit other different types of relationships, and thus, other Bonding Patterns. On the contrary, a relationship between two Aware Egos provides enough confidence to enable each person to form a wide range of relationships appropriate to different circumstances and situations.

However, in a parallel fashion, if this is a primary, fundamental couple relationship, such as we have described to this point, it does not easily tolerate any transfer to another person or other thing. This would change its nature, or more precisely, it would change the primary relationship – which is not to say that this is always a bad thing in itself. Once again, what we need to ask ourselves is not what we are doing, but rather, who is doing it. "Who is changing the primary relationship? The Aware Ego? Or a Sub-Personality, which is acting without consideration for the others?"

The "captivating third", which has just undermined the primary relationship for its own benefit, can take many forms, for example:

- A very dear friend (male or female), who is the final refuge, to whom we tell all our secrets, even those our partner doesn't know; we even share private details about our partner.
- A lover or mistress, who fulfills a need unmet in the primary relationship, even though that need has never been communicated or discussed between both partners.
- Work, business, travel.
- A pet, "the only one who accepts me as I am!"
- Cars, computers, reading, a hobby – in short, anything that consumes our energy and attention.

We must mention here one "third element" that is particularly enthralling because of its immediate appeal: a child. The birth of a child very often brings about a change in the nature of the primary relationship between the two partners, as one or other of the parents bonds more closely with the newborn than with the partner. This change can be profoundly disturbing; it brings with it a significant backlash when the child, having grown up, heads out into the world, leaving the parents to the task of rebuilding their relationship. It is important that parents be able to communicate their experiences for there to be an Aware Ego belonging to the couple which manages their relationship, rather than just some patriarchal or matriarchal voice imposing its rule.

THE AGING PROCESS

Jung identifies two major stages in the unfolding of human existence:

- In the first stage, we settle into life: we must make our way, earn a living, create a home and have children to support us in our old age. To accomplish these things, we mainly use our preferred functions; our Auto-Pilot is at work most of the time, even if all our efforts are aimed at developing an Aware Ego.
- In the second stage, we seek completeness, and we integrate the aspects of our personality which we have not made use of thus far. This is the time where we "individuate", where we become autonomous, whole individuals.

Two phases characterize this period:

- midlife, with its accompanying "crisis", and
- acquisition of some degree of wisdom.

Midlife and Crisis

The change, or perhaps even crisis, of midlife is a well-known phenomenon, and literature is rife with examples: "My goodness! Men and women succumbing to temptation and leaving family and station to venture out with a younger partner...." These clichés reveal, however, a reality that we are able to comprehend when we look at the dynamics of the psyche.

During this phase of life, a dual phenomenon manifests itself:

- On one hand, the Auto-Pilot is typically slowing down, discovering its limitations, as we have already seen in several different examples. This may be because after having exerted so much effort, it is exhausted, or because it no longer feels comfortable in the changing environment. At this point, the children are grown, preparing to leave the family nest if they haven't done so already. In our professional life, we are able to see the trajectory of our career and extrapolate the future quite clearly. At age 20, we might have the makings of a five-star general; at 45 we know more or less what rank we can hope to attain, and we also know that five-star generals are few and far between.
- On the other hand, the shadow functions are clamoring to be heard, particularly the inferior function. We will observe this phenomenon in relation to professional mobility, which we will examine later. It shows up in other areas of life as well: family, culture, art, leisure, and hobbies.

The appearance of the inferior function can occur gradually so that we are not aware of it: the change takes place little by little, and we suddenly notice it, the way one day our gray hairs catch our attention in the mirror.

This is how we arrive at a point where we can say "Well, I'm not going to do that anymore", or "Oh well, no point getting worked up over that kind of person anymore!" The change can also show up in new interests: "Now I can do things I wasn't able to do when I was younger", for example, enjoying spending time with one's grandchildren (for someone who has Introverted Thinking as dominant) or enjoying moments of solitude to think quietly (for someone who has Extraverted Feeling as dominant).

However, the inferior function can also manifest in a much more abrupt, intrusive fashion, as we described in the section dealing with function dynamics. These manifestations can be even more violent if the Auto-Pilot has been strongly repressing the shadow side.

The table below summarizes some of the transformations that can occur; the intention is to alert everyone to the changes which may be operating within.

Table 5.1 – Function Reversal at Midlife

Dominant to *Inferior*	Potential New Interests	Excessive Shadow Signs
Extraverted Sensing *Introverted Intuiting*	Long-term strategizing; vision of the future Reading novels Spiritual research	Blind mysticism, esoterism Fear of the future Excessive planning
Introverted Sensing *Extraverted Intuiting*	Curiosity about new things Developing sense of creativity; Contacts, encounters, exchanges	Dispersal, agitation Loss of contact with reality Imagination running wild, unrealistic
Extraverted Intuiting *Introverted Sensing*	Making the most of past experience Respect for tradition; Grounded in the past	Obsession over detail Rigidity, procedures Hypochondriasis, cyclothymia
Introverted Intuiting *Extraverted Sensing*	Enjoying "the now" Pleasure, improvisation; Relaxing handicrafts and projects	All forms of sensorial excess Neophyte activism Dilettantism
Extraverted Thinking *Introverted Feeling*	Active listening, empathy Spirituality, deeper meaning; Valuing beauty, harmony	Oversensitivity Sentimentality Self-pity Withdrawal, depression
Introverted Thinking *Extraverted Feeling*	Hospitality, social warmth Widening social circle Cultural and/or social involvement	Overzealousness Extremism Need to do good for others Emotional blind spots
Extraverted Feeling *Introverted Thinking*	Philosophical reflection, critical thinking Reading, intellectual stimulation Solitude	Negativity, self-destructive criticism Isolationism, withdrawal Cynicism, discouragement
Introverted Feeling *Extraverted Thinking*	Organization, methodical approach Assertiveness, acceptance of responsibilities Public statement of abilities	Aggressivity, brutality Authoritarianism Revenge on people and things

Growing Older… Growing Wiser?

Growing older is inevitable; growing wiser is the challenge that awaits us once we have progressed through the preceding stages. Additionally, improvements in lifespan and healthcare have made this a much more important stage of life than it was only a few decades ago. It is a new age, still relatively unknown, a form of "*terra incognita*" that can last 20, 30, or even 40 years!

Which is to say that, in terms of our psychic life, the journey is far from over!

We will outline some possible characteristics of this period, assuming a favorable outlook:

- The Aware Ego takes up a greater place, and the Auto-Pilot doesn't try to take control; decisions are made more slowly but more carefully.
- Projection, and therefore judging, occurs far less frequently; tolerance increases gradually as the opposite poles are integrated.
- The most hidden aspects of personality, the ones we have labelled "the shadow of the shadow" become more appealing; unexpected behaviors occur.
- Pressure for external success diminishes to the benefit of inner exploration and growth; new activities are taken up for their intrinsic interest, in a noncompetitive manner.
- The inner quest and participation in the world around us are as systole and diastole, keeping a rhythm between the inner Self and the outer world.

This notion of wisdom is not the sage meditating on the mountaintop in blissful contentment, but rather a notion based on the conciliation of opposites. Wisdom and madness coexist. And to be sure, Bonding Patterns, although much less common, will certainly still arise, reminding us that "Man is neither angel nor beast, and misfortune would have it that whoever wants to play at being an angel will act like a beast!"[12]

CAREER AND PROFESSIONAL MOBILITY

If life as a couple and family preoccupations take up a large part of our life, professional activity makes up for at least as much, and hence, the importance attached to the choice of career and working conditions.

---

[12] Pascal†, *Pensées* VI, p. 358

It will come as no surprise by now that the one question in particular that Intelligence of Self raises in terms of professional guidance is: "Who in me is choosing the career, or the job?" Of course, this "someone" is one of the Parts within us, and we must clarify the different voices which wish to be heard in order to permit the Aware Ego to emerge and demonstrate its faculty of discernment.

Who Chooses Our Career?

If we consider psychic development as it is described by the typological approach, this question means different things if we are asking a 20-year old or a 40-year-old.

The First Career

Who, which part of ourselves, chooses this first career?

Although it is far from always being so, it would appear logical to choose the first career from the area of preferred psychic functions. For example, an Si/Te (ISTJ) will focus rather naturally on careers requiring discipline and accuracy, such as accounting and jurisprudence. In contrast, an Ne/Fi (ENFP) will be drawn to professions which require imagination and contact with others, such as public relations or advertising. A great number of authors[13] have successfully established links between psychological type and choice of profession.

It is, however, out of the question to use these correlations to directly infer a choice of a profession. This principle requires us to make several comments:

- The link between psychological type and profession indicates a spontaneous affinity, a natural facility in a given professional context; it does not indicate aptitude.
- The career choice must be placed in the context of the company in which the work is performed: an accounting job in a petroleum company or with Greenpeace are two entirely different things.

---

[13] See Bibliography, Shaubhut and Thompson

- A number of other factors must also be considered: level of education, established adaptation strategies, aptitude, job openings, fortune/luck....

Which is to say that with all these constraints, the Aware Ego will find it even more difficult to emerge, as a significant number of others will also want to speak in its place – often parents, but also teachers, some counselors, and all well-intentioned individuals who "know what is best for the other".

For those who must make this choice, some voices are commonly heard:

- The Obedient Child: Parents and educators are the keepers of knowledge, and this individual has acquired the habit of obeying without discussion. In any case, everything works out just fine – the career the child wants is the same as Dad's or Mom's.
- The Rebel who always takes the opposite direction, thus continuing to be under the influence of another.
- The Opportunist ('opportunity makes the thief'): the first good-paying job will fit the bill.
- The Responsible: this individual does what he must, no questions asked.

If the choice of career is not made by the Aware Ego, there will most likely be a boomerang effect which manifests in the form of boredom, stress, regret, remorse, or subpar performance.

> Philip Ni/Te (INTJ) began his career in a bank, in charge of creating new products. This fits well with his psychological type, as it is characterized by efficient innovation and what's more, the pay was good. But having completed his task, Philip found himself in a typical banking environment where he was utterly bored. A well-intentioned mentor encouraged him to stay, explaining that after 40 years, the work would get interesting. Philip didn't have that much patience and decided not to wait around to find out....

Fortunately, our first career choice is not irreversible, and we are permitted to make subsequent adjustments.

Career Change

There are two main causes for career change:

- An external event: restructuring, transfer, job loss....
- An inner need for change due to personal evolution and growth.

In actual fact, if the first career is chosen from fields related to the preferred functions, it is quite predictable that as the individual develops and integrates the tertiary and inferior functions, there will be an accompanying progression of professional interests. This is why we see individuals who have, to this point, followed an unswerving career path suddenly showing what appears, at first glance, to be a very surprising interest in a new sector. It is important to try to find a balance between the two voices:

- the Responsible, which wants to maximize profit and minimize risk, and
- the Daredevil, which wants to get away from what it increasingly considers to be a straightjacket.

External events and internal change can also very well combine and reinforce one another, as the example of Roger illustrates. The orientation session transcribed here has obviously been shortened. The interview progresses in accordance with the process of Voice Dialogue, which we will explain in more detail in Chapter 7.

Roger's New Direction

Roger, type Si/Te (ISTJ), is organized, methodical, and conscientious. After a 20-year career in a large company, his last promotion led him to a significant failure. He therefore took advantage of a retirement plan and left with a good payout, but he feels lost because he doesn't know what to do with himself.

Roger: "So I guess I'm not even too sure what happened. I've always been good at my work – I had a brilliant career – everyone always sought me out on account of my competence, so I never really had any doubts. But then I had some unexpected difficulties that I couldn't figure out, and that's still a problem, because now I don't really know what to do. I'm being asked to prove that I can be creative, but that's not really my thing. I know I can be very efficient, but only in a support position. On my own, I'm not sure which way to go."

Coach: "If I understand correctly, your talent is in your efficiency and methodical approach."

Roger: "Yes, you could say that!"

Coach: "Could I speak to the part of you that is efficient and organized?"

Roger: "No problem – that part is always available."

Coach: "Where would it seat itself in the room?"

Roger gets up and goes to stand in a corner at the back of the room; from there, he can see everything without being at the forefront. He remains standing, with his arms crossed.

Coach: "It's a great pleasure to meet you. Roger just told me that you are a very organized and methodical person...."

Roger, as his Sub-Personality, the Organizer:

"Yes, right, that's true. You know, without a method, you don't get anywhere. As for myself, I really don't like to be at center stage, but I know how to plan, organize, and get things rolling. I'm the good soldier."

Coach: "I know that Roger is feeling quite lost right now – he just told me so. What do you think about this? How do you see things?"

Roger, as his Sub-Personality, the Organizer:

Becoming Who You Are with the Intelligence of Self

"Hmmm. I don't know! I know how to get things done, but I don't lead. It's his job to tell me. What frightens me is that he doesn't seem to know either. I feel like a high-performance race car left rusting in a parking lot.

Coach: "Well let's ask Roger what he thinks."

Roger, seated in the center where he began the session:

"I really get it, about this race car going to rust. It's a real mess and it makes me sad. I actually feel like an idiot – I feel like hiding.

Coach: "Nothing is stopping you from doing that here. Where would you like to hide?"

Roger goes to the other side of the room and sits on a sofa. He curls up in ball with his eyes closed and stays that way for a while.

Coach: "Yes...."

The Part that is Hiding speaks very slowly, haltingly:

"It's hard to say…. I feel things very strongly. I need time. That guy over there is always in a rush, always ready to start, but I need some quiet time to figure out what I feel like doing…."

He remains silent for a long moment. Then of his own accord, he returns to the central chair, looking like a new man, with his eyes wide open.

Coach: "What is happening?"

Roger: "Something just clicked when I was over there on the sofa. I realized that I have always been at the beck and call of people who did the thinking for me and who told me to be serious. But in fact, I haven't ever really done what I enjoyed – and what I want to do isn't all that serious, obviously, but in fact, it is very important to me. And so, I would like to have been a clown so I could do something for sick kids. But in actual fact, I could put my skills to work to support their cause, and that would bring me something that's missing, something that I really need."

Some observations on the process:

- Roger's Auto-Pilot corresponds to his preferred psychic functions: Introverted Sensing – his sense of duty and work well done, and Extraverted Thinking – order and organization. These two functions have made him into a top-notch achiever, but he hasn't yet gotten in touch with the entire side of himself that holds his inner motivation, Introverted Feeling (Fi).
- However competent his Auto-Pilot might be, it was not able to cope with two new situations arising one after the other which did not fall into its area of competency:
    - unexpected situations in his career which caused his failure,
    - followed by the loss of his job and the resulting blank slate now lying before him.
- Roger is so accustomed to his Auto-Pilot dutifully jumping into action to meet the requests of others that he has difficulty getting his own bearings and understanding his own wishes.
- When he is overcome by his feelings and goes to sit on the sofa, he is able to begin to listen to his tertiary function, Introverted Feeling. It is aware of the priorities, but it needs time. It functions in a manner that is radically different from Extraverted Thinking, and it could not play its role while Roger remained so strongly plugged into the external world.
- Having been able to contact his tertiary function, Roger begins to have lots of new ideas which are "apparently not very serious" (when viewed by his Si/Te side), and these ideas arise from his inferior function, Extraverted Intuiting. This is a very common phenomenon; the tertiary function is the route to access the inferior function. How does that occur? It depends on each individual – there is no directory cataloguing the relationships between the tertiary and inferior functions. But experience has shown that if we enter deeply enough into the energy of the tertiary, we can each find our own

- unique path which opens a way toward the inferior. The tertiary acts as a springboard.
- Having experienced two completely opposite poles (the "good soldier" and Introverted Feeling, the function closely linked to his soul), and having felt the appearance of the third pole (the creative capacity of Extraverted Intuiting), Roger's Aware Ego begins to emerge and finds much more choice for his new career direction. A breakthrough has occurred. He will find it easy to roll out an action plan that he can entrust to his Auto-Pilot, which has the talent for such tasks.

MANAGEMENT POSITIONS

By "management", we are referring here to any position which requires responsibility or leadership in an organization. To be clear, this goes from the position of CEO of a multinational corporation to the owner of the local corner store, from the Secretary of Education to the parent registering a child at school. The term "manager" is generally tied to professional activity – and associated synonyms are "executive, decision-maker, administrator, boss, supervisor". But each one of us performs this function in both our professional and private spheres, whether we exercise authority over many millions of individuals (the Secretary of Education) or over only one individual (the parent) or over ourselves alone. In truth, it seems to us that it may be more difficult and more complicated to manage a family than to manage a large company. The size of the organization certainly increases the number of people a manager can impact, but it also dilutes the sense of individual responsibility.

Who is Making the Decisions?

If this question about decision-making is aimed at the manager in particular, as it is one of his main roles, if not the principal role, it also falls to each individual at all times. In fact, everything is a decision, including not deciding. Except that we cannot always make all our decisions by consulting with our Aware Ego. If we tried, we would most likely find ourselves, at dinnertime, still hesitating over the choice of tea or coffee for breakfast. The Auto-Pilot is perfectly skilled at resolving a great number of questions that are not worth our consideration.

The practical question thus becomes: "When do we unplug the Auto-Pilot?" or in other words, "When do we need to awaken our true pilot, the Aware Ego, and put it into the driver's seat?"

Two principal types of cases can arise:

- In temporary circumstances – the Auto-Pilot is not adapted to the particular situation.
- In general circumstances – the Auto-Pilot, in any case, needs to be adjusted on a regular basis.

The "Auto-Pilot" is Not Adapted to the Situation

There are two main reasons which explain its lack of adaptation:

The situation has changed; the problem must be formulated in different terms.

> Yvonne's firm beliefs leave her adamantly opposed to divorce, and her Auto-Pilot strongly advises her to avoid contact with divorced people – she "excommunicates" them. And then her daughter gets divorced and remarries! Yvonne's maternal love comes into conflict with her Auto-Pilot, and she must find a way to readjust.
>
> In terms of economics, there is a constant need to diversify in order to adapt and survive in a world that is perpetually changing.
>
> Otherwise we end up like the unfortunate industrialist owner of a broom-making company who was deeply attached to the quality of his horsehair brooms. When nylon arrived on the market, his Auto-Pilot resisted; the company went bankrupt, and he committed suicide.

The problem falls outside of the competence of the Auto-Pilot.

> Victor, a time management specialist, teaches others to be like he is: punctual, organized, methodical. His priorities are evaluated in an impersonal, objective manner. When his eldest son, typologically very different, becomes a teenager, Victor realizes that there is a need to strengthen their connection. His overworked Auto-Pilot does some planning: "I see that my son requires a greater paternal presence. Therefore, I am going to change my schedule and clear a two-hour window of time for him on Saturday afternoons."

Let's hope his son feels flattered by such an "effort".

The difficulty here is not in understanding why the Auto-Pilot is inadequate, but rather in realizing that it cannot manage every issue, and that a solution cannot be found simply by letting it work harder. When a prescription is not working, why double the dose?

If there were miracle cures, we would know of them. However, we can make some observations:

- It is useless to try to argue with an Auto-Pilot that has the bit in its teeth. This will only strengthen its conviction and lead to a painful dispute.
- When the pressure has lessened and we are consulted, we can diplomatically suggest that perhaps a change of strategy would be appropriate. But take care – the Auto-Pilot is very wary of attempts at psychological manipulation. Asking sanctimoniously "Who is speaking?" would be like waving one's hand inside a hornets' nest.
- The only real solution is for the person to realize on his own that the Operating Ego has limits, and that it is not all-powerful. But before that can occur, we generally hit a few bumps along the way.

> Gilbert is a senior executive in a large company. His type Te/Ni (ENTJ) naturally predisposes him for leadership; his program of studies in a large engineering school opened the doors for him. Unfortunately, Gilbert exemplifies the worst traits of the dominant function Extraverted Thinking; he behaves in an authoritative, even brutal manner. Obsessed with achieving the objective, he shows no consideration for his collaborators, and he bullies them in order to "get the most out of them", or so he says.

His superiors have pointed out his faults, to no avail. This goes on until his career peters out, and he is moved into a dead-end position. A short time later, a 360° evaluation[14] of leadership style is planned for his old department. His former boss decides to give him one last chance by including him on the list of executives to be evaluated.

As we might well expect, the results, delivered to Gilbert and to the coach who knows him well, are disastrous. The coach arranges a follow-up meeting to discuss the report. The encounter begins with the following dialogue.

- Gilbert says without preamble: "Listen, I'm really disappointed. Your system really doesn't work."
- Coach, quite surprised: "Oh? And why not?"
- Gilbert: "Well, you've seen the results, haven't you?"
- Coach: "Yes, and I'm actually here to talk to you about them."
- Gilbert: "But they are all wrong!"
- Coach: "How so?"
- Gilbert: "Well look – all the questions got mixed up. I marked my answers with an asterisk, and the results don't match at all. Your computer messed up completely. You'll have to redo the whole thing, man."
- Coach, after taking a moment to pull himself together: "Gilbert, let me explain. Each question corresponds to a specific theme, and the themes were the purpose of the evaluation. When you completed the questionnaire, the questions were mixed up to make the questionnaire less transparent. But in the report, each question is clustered around its related theme. That's why the numbering system is not the same."
- Gilbert, after a much longer silence: "Do you mean that it's not your computer that is at fault?"
- Coach: "That's correct."

---

[14] A 360° evaluation consists of the same questionnaire being completed by the person being evaluated, by his superior and, anonymously, by coworkers and colleagues. The perceptions are then compared.

The ensuing silence would fill several pages. And then Gilbert got down to work.

The Auto-Pilot Needs to be Adjusted on a Regular Basis

An engineer from a heavy industrial steelmaking company one day commented: "When we begin to treat humans as well as we treat machines, we will have made great strides forward". At first glance, this is a shocking statement. "What?! Treat men like machines?! How shocking!" But with experience, we can appreciate the validity of the comment. No engineer or technician would ever neglect the maintenance of a machine. If this were to occur, the consequences would be soon obvious. Most of us probably make arrangements for the oil change and maintenance of our vehicle, more or less at the recommended times.

But when do we ever think about stepping back, about analyzing our own way of functioning, about evaluating the results, or calling into question whether it is still suitable? Not very often. Very fortunately, the human psyche is more flexible than a machine, and it adapts better, whether we are aware of this or not. But unfortunately, this same flexibility enables us to delay our analysis...until the day that things are so bluntly put before us that we can no longer avoid it. And at that point, the cost will most likely be higher than if we had simply anticipated and made the inevitable changes.

It is therefore important to become aware – in a lucid, intentional manner – of one's Auto-Pilot, and what it can lead us to. This is, in fact, Intelligence of Self. Chapters 7 and 8 of this book offer the reader ways to become "intelligent" before it is too late.

Who is Leading?

In the exercise of authority, there are two considerations:

- The "natural" qualities of the leader, which justify his influence over the group.
- The agreement of the group, which gives its approval of the leader's role.

These two aspects are complementary and equally necessary. The theory of Intelligence of Self sheds new light on this.

The "Aware Ego" of the Leader

The most important quality of the leader is his ability to exercise authority from the Aware Ego. There are three reasons for this:

1. A decision made in the Aware Ego avoids any backlash because the opposite polarities were considered. The violent swinging from hard left to hard right, which negatively affects many organizations, is thus minimized or even eliminated. This greases the gears and spares the resources.
2. The Aware Ego is in it for the long haul; it is a long-term team member. The Auto-Pilot can generate momentum but can also drive straight into a brick wall. The Aware Ego is less of a cheerleader and more of a steady drummer.
3. From the Aware Ego, leadership can be modified to suit different parameters, such as:
   - team members' personalities,
   - their level of autonomy, motivation and competency, and
   - the context in which the team is working.

Situational Management and Intelligence of Self

The theory of Situational Leadership developed by Paul Hersey and Kenneth Blanchard[15] can be married perfectly to the typological approach, as each of the styles these authors propose corresponds to a typological profile.

Leadership style "Telling" (Sensing/Thinking, ST): this style is focused on accomplishment of the task through rational, coherent organization. The leader defines the roles, and the chain of command is solidly structured. This style corresponds in general to "Sensing" and "Thinking" types.

---

[15] Hersey, Blanchard, Johnson. *Management of Organizational Behavior Leading Human Resources*, and Seminar Notes.

Leadership style "Selling" (Sensing/Feeling, SF): this style is focused on accomplishment of the task but depends more on the solid network of relationships than on a rational structuring. This style corresponds in general to "Sensing" and "Feeling" types.

Leadership style "Participating" (Intuiting/Feeling, NF): guidance is based on a shared vision of the goal to achieve. The leader is more of a team facilitator. This is typically the style of "Intuiting" and "Feeling" type individuals.

Leadership style "Delegating" (Intuiting/Thinking, NT): the leader projects the vision and acts as project leader. Team members are given responsibilities over which they have a high degree of autonomy. This is typically the style of "Intuiting" and "Thinking" type individuals.

The talent of a leader is to be able to use these different styles as needed. In order to do this, a leader must unite his own opposites, which is the exclusive role of the Aware Ego. But this is not easy! Here for example, is Bernard's experience:

> Bernard is type Si/Te (ISTJ). He excelled in engineering in a first-class institution and began working right away for a very prestigious firm. His career progressed without a hitch until he was about 40 years old. At the point when a top management path is opening up for him, he is told that in order to move up, he must change his leadership style. To assist him with this, his firm proposes coaching sessions.
>
> Bernard's first challenge is to understand what is happening. What has he done wrong to be prevented from moving into management when previously, his work has been well regarded, and he's completed each stage without difficulty? He hasn't done anything wrong. But what helped him succeed to this point is about to slow him down.
>
> This is because Bernard manages his team through personal competency in each domain that his collaborators work in. For him, the boss must know things better than each of his team members. His function of Introverted Sensing, a veritable database of knowledge, coupled with his great intelligence, have enabled him to meet this demand; however, he has had to pay the price of an ever-increasing workload. At the start of the coaching, Bernard

is working on average 12 hours per day, 6 days per week. He takes a little time off on Sunday mornings.... For Bernard, his Operating Ego is like a bullet train moving at top speed. Up until now, his strategy has always been to increase the power. But he is at his limit: the locomotive can't go faster; the cars can't follow; there is a major risk of derailment. In fact, he has just had a little cardiac event that has made him ponder things over.

And this might also just be the reason his wife has left him, taking the children. Lucid to the point of cynicism, he confesses: "At the beginning, it suited me just fine – I was able to work in peace...." But now he is suffering from a lack of a close relationships. Well, what do you expect – a bullet train isn't really intended for social outings. For that, you'd need to slow down, stop in all the small stations. But it's not all that easy to stop a bullet train. When he is finally able to do that, Bernard will be able to integrate the opposite poles, Ne/Fi (ENFP) Extraverted Intuiting/Introverted Feeling.

THE AWARE EGO AND POLITICS

The approach suggested by Intelligence of Self can be applied at the societal level. This was illustrated by Hal and Sidra Stone in their analysis[16] of the events of September 11th, 2001.

In fact, the principal cultural traits of a society are comparable to Sub-Personalities, and these collective Sub-Personalities behave in a way which is similar to what we described for individual Sub-Personalities. There remains only the task of ensuring that a collective Aware Ego emerge; this is undoubtedly more difficult than for the individual Aware Ego.

Principles

The "laws" which we enumerated in Part I take on a particular power and nuance at the collective level. In actuality, the phenomenon of polarization comes into full play, and we are quick to demonize in others the very aspects we don't wish to acknowledge in ourselves.

---

[16] *See Bibliography: Newsletters, October 15th and November 18th 2001*

This process of exclusion occurs in four steps:

1. In a given culture, for every dominant polarity, there is, within that culture, a corresponding opposite polarity which is devalued or rejected.
2. The rejected polarity is cherished by another culture, which in turn, rejects the dominant polarity of the first culture.
3. Both cultures are convinced of their absolute righteousness, and each one judges the other.
4. In the name of proclaiming its values, each group feels entitled to go to war against the other in order to ensure the victory of their viewpoint.

G-strings and burkas

We will begin with an example that has been discussed extensively – not to take sides, obviously - but to reveal the mechanism at work.

Western society favors the expression of the rights of the individual. Among these, a woman's freedom to choose her clothing (which is very directly linked to moral freedom, sexual freedom, and the status of women) is prominently featured. This freedom is in large part a liberation; not so long ago young girls were still prohibited from wearing pants in certain schools. But these days, the female body is unveiled, not only in images, but also in reality – one need only notice the latest teenage fashion: mid-riff T-shirt with plunging neckline and ultra-lowrise jeans.

Modesty and propriety, values which were highly valued some decades ago, are rejected, or might even make our scantily clad teenager laugh! There is a very fine line between what is private and what is public.

In an opposite vein, other societies make female modesty a cardinal virtue of their culture. A woman is veiled when in public "to keep herself for her husband", as we were told one day in Amman by our veiled guide, who was, furthermore, well educated and modern in her outlook. And if there was, at one time, a decline in the wearing of the veil, that is no longer the case. In this context, a half-dressed woman is a provocative hussy. The sight of such a woman is not tolerated, except in certain, well-defined contexts, such as a Middle Eastern "belly dance" show.

We therefore have the impression that some women are covering up, using all the clothing that the others are taking off, or that some are undressing just as much as others are hiding. With this developing polarization, the judgments are well underway:

- Western women are "sluts"; men have no honor, and
- Muslim women are slaves; men are macho pigs

At this stage, complaints, protests, excommunications, condemnations, and fatwas are flying. The hunt is on: holy wars always begin with a disparagement of those who "dishonor humanity", which is to say, **our** concept of humanity.

In fact, the question is not deciding if it is better to wear a G-string or a burka; once again, the question we should be asking ourselves is "Who in me is wearing the G-string or the burka?" Is it the Aware Ego or a primary Sub-Personality that cannot do anything else and that hasn't integrated the opposite pole?

As with personal development work, the final battle occurs for everyone with the reintegration of the opposite pole, which, on a cultural and political level, is no small feat. And yet, we can easily believe that all the conflicts tearing apart our planet are caused by an absentee Aware Ego, both at the individual and the collective levels.

This is the reason we believe that the approach which we are suggesting has a universal scope: any awakening of the Aware Ego, no matter how slight, can only improve human existence.

In summary

The process of the Aware Ego is a constant quest, belonging to all stages of existence, from childhood to our golden years, in all domains, from life in a couple, to our professional activities. It requires vigilance, lucidity, and willpower.

It is not easy to undertake this quest alone: at more challenging moments, it can become extremely difficult. At these moments, the help of a third party can be helpful, and it may be time to consider seeking help from a specialist, coach, or therapist.

6

INTELLIGENCE OF SELF, INTELLIGENCE OF THE COACH

If we wished to reduce the Intelligence of Self approach to its essence, it would be this one simple question: "Who is speaking?"

Who in me is speaking at any given moment? The Operating Ego? A dominant Sub-Personality? An unknown part of myself showing up unannounced? The Aware Ego?

Who is speaking among all of us when we are in a group? What Bonding Patterns are our different parts playing out?

Simple? Not really, because the question can't be asked by just anyone, at just any time.

We can ask ourselves in our leisure moments. That's a very good exercise. But it's not easy to do this, especially under duress, and it's even more difficult to answer. The Operating Ego is all too happy to offer answers to all the questions, even the ones we don't ask.

A third party can ask this question, but not under just any circumstances, otherwise it could quickly turn into psychological manipulation to cause problems or to gain the upper hand over another person. Interrupting someone to ask "Who is speaking?" is an outrageous way to shut them up or to provoke a heated response!

So this must be done under specific conditions, which can be found in places dedicated to self-development, coaching, or therapy. Experience shows that it is difficult to accomplish this work alone. It is certainly not impossible, but the help of a trained third party may help an individual advance more rapidly and further than they would progress on their own.

Intelligence of Self is more than just a method that we apply to others without looking at ourselves; it is a way to look at ourselves and the world. It is a way to feel, to understand, and to act, and for this reason, it enables us to look at the job of coach in a very specific light. In this particular instance, we want the shoemaker to be well shod!

By applying the principles of Intelligence of Self to the job of coaching, we are attempting to hit three birds with one stone; our goals are:

- To help coaches enrich their practice.
- To show future coaches what this self-development approach looks like, and what they can expect from it.
- To offer an example so that its principles can be applied in other fields.

Coaching in the light of Intelligence of Self requires essentially that we step back in order to be able to coach from our Aware Ego, and that we be able to hold the tension between the opposites.

We will consider these elements in order:

- The coach's posture, a key element.
- The way this posture appears at different stages of the coaching process.
- The relationship between coach and client.

THE COACH'S POSTURE: WHO IS COACHING?

This question cuts to the heart of the matter, and in a way, all other questions are related to it. Coaches are in charge of the Aware Ego, starting first with their own Aware Ego Process. In other words, they attempt to embrace the opposite poles that appear at a particular time, in a given coaching session, because their role is to help facilitate the experience of the opposing Selves within the client.

Who is coaching, or rather who wants to coach? This is asking which part of oneself, which voice? The one that wants to get results? The one that has a goal for the client? The one that is impatient to see progress? The one who is bored to tears? The one who is coaching because "you have to make a living one way or another"? The one who wants to help the client feel better? The one who likes to find quick fixes?

In other words, when the coach starts a session, he is no more alone than the client! There are entire families of Sub-Personalities that are going to meet and come into resonance

The coach's "role" consists of first identifying these different voices within himself and holding himself centered as much as possible throughout the entire session. This is what enables him to interact with each of the client's Sub-Personalities without locking into any one of them, and in this way the coach awakens the Aware Ego Process of the client.

The 8 Functions and the Coach

This is easier said than done, of course.

To help us with this, the typology offers once again a reference chart that gives us a good overview. We will return to the eight functions-attitudes, which form opposing pairs: Se-Ni, Si-Ne, Te-Fi, Ti-Fe. In each case, it is the Aware Ego which must embrace the opposites. What does this mean for the coach?

Extraverted Sensing – Introverted Intuiting (Se-Ni)

Extraverted Sensing is the propensity to be present in the moment. It likes to go with the flow, always ready to react to the smallest change. It excels in finding practical solutions to immediate problems.

For example, it enables the coach to:

- Notice all the changes occurring within the client: changes of position, tone of voice, rising or falling energy levels.
- Remain interested in each Sub-Personality, in the pleasure of the interaction, without an agenda, experiencing the moment.
- Enjoy seeing simple, practical, even game-like solutions arising in an unexpected fashion.

If it is the only voice at the controls, the coach risks:

- Reacting in the short term, without an overall perspective on the client's issues.
- Being satisfied with minor changes of behavior without being able to see the overall picture.

Introverted Intuiting is the propensity to perceive the connections underlying different elements and to bring them together in a long-term, global vision. It excels in developing strategies and scenarios.

For example, it enables the coach to:

- Make connections between a variety of data to set up hypotheses which help organize the session.
- Easily access the memorized charts which explain what the client may be experiencing.
- Step back to gain an overall perspective of what is happening in the session.

If it is the only voice at the controls, the coach risks:

- Being satisfied with an abstract explanation without any practical application.
- Appearing distant, unengaging.

Introverted Sensing – Extraverted Intuiting (Si-Ne)

Introverted Sensing is the propensity to record experiences and to compare them to previous experiences. It excels in doing things methodically, accurately, and in the collection and organization of precise details.

For example, it enables the coach to:

- Make associations between what the client may have said or done at different steps of the process; have a clear record of the clients' history.

- Ask relevant questions to deepen a particular point or to come back to reality.
- Avoid approximations and confusing areas; stay specific and maintain the focus on the client's goals.

If it is the only voice at the controls, the coach risks:

- Becoming an interrogator and focusing on a single, unrelated point.
- Becoming limited in perspective; not helping the client broaden his point of view.

Extraverted Intuiting is the propensity to produce a continual fountain of ideas and new possibilities. It excels in rebounding, in finding novel solutions even in apparently dead-end situations.

For example, it enables the coach to:

- Imagine, in an unrestricted manner, all solutions, even those that appear to be impossible.
- Get off the beaten path and out of well-traveled ruts to encourage resilience and new discoveries.
- Demonstrate optimism, because the world is new every morning, and anything is possible.

If it is the only voice at the controls, the coach risks:

- Losing a sense of direction in the work; going off on a tangent and not making progress.
- Getting lost in the client's dreams without coming back to reality or discovering practical actions.

Extraverted Thinking – Introverted Feeling (Te-Fi)

Extraverted Thinking is the propensity to express a thought logically, methodically, and efficiently. It excels in organizing, making action plans, structuring strategies and putting them into practice.

For example, it enables the coach to:

- Help the client clearly see the options by being specific about the different possible options.
- Clarify the goals and the evaluation criteria and establish priorities.
- Provide a method which supports the established action plan and organize its implementation over time.

If it is the only voice at the controls, the coach risks:

- Making decisions for the client, telling him what needs doing, not considering his doubts, or even becoming impatient with them.
- Greatly oversimplifying a situation in the hope of reaching a conclusion quickly.

Introverted Feeling is the propensity to create harmony around deeply felt personal values. It excels in deep understanding of others, and in centering itself around essential values, even in the most complicated situations.

For example, it enables the coach to:

- Come into resonance with the client, to be, in a way, his "loudspeaker".
- Take the time required to support the client who is letting a decision "ripen" to maturity.
- Position himself comfortably at the heart of the issue and ask the fundamental questions without being put off by nonissues or avoidance strategies.

If it is the only voice at the controls, the coach risks:

- Being a victim of his own values and trying to influence the client indirectly.
- Fearing the client's moment of decision and delaying it for as long as possible in fear of superficiality.

Extraverted Feeling – Introverted Thinking (Fe-Ti)

Extraverted Feeling is the propensity to create harmony around values that are shared by the group. It excels in organizing relationships between others, and in supporting them moving toward a common goal.

For example, it enables the coach to:

- Be warm and welcoming toward the client and have enthusiasm for his projects.
- Do whatever it takes to make the client feel at ease and spend considerable energy doing so.
- Support the client through the coach's generosity, dynamism, and empathy.

If it is the only voice at the controls, the coach risks:

- Believing he knows better than the client what is suitable, wanting to do well by the client in spite of the client's own desires, or confusing empathy and friendship to such an extent that a friend is gained and a client is lost.
- Conforming to social values and suffering when the client does not share them.

Introverted Thinking is the propensity to find a rational explanation for everything through a continual questioning. It excels in stepping back, criticizing, determining priorities.

For example, it enables the coach to:

- Take a step back from the client and not be "pulled into the vacuum" of his system.
- Not be "taken in" by the client; demonstrate perceptiveness and critical thinking skills.
- Ensure the client does not delude himself, impose limits.

If it is the only voice at the controls, the coach risks:

- Viewing the client as an interesting "case" without feeling enough understanding or empathy for the person.
- Getting lost in theoretical analysis with a view to publishing an interesting article while forgetting the client's existence.

The Coach's Sub-Personalities

In terms of Sub-Personalities, we must once again identify which one is at the controls without us knowing, in order to keep it at a distance, and that way we encourage the other pole to emerge. We can spot a few common Sub-Personalities, although for each individual, the experience is always unique.

In the next section we will use terms which our clients chose spontaneously to identify their Sub-Personalities, including some terms having a negative connotation, for example, the Loser. We emphasize that no particular part in itself is "a loser" (or selfish, or lazy, etc.); there is simply a part of us that is judged by another part to be a loser. This may even appear to be true, especially since we don't let this voice speak up because it's reputed to be... a loser. In the course of the work, one comes to understand that the supposed Loser part is only like this in respect to the criteria of the Operating Ego, and in fact, this part reveals that it actually offers us a richness or gift that represents a 180-degree contrast to the judgments of the Operating Ego.

The Loser and the Almighty

This pair of Sub-Personalities is often encountered; it is typical not only of the job of coach but also of many helping professions in which, without going to extremes, the professional can swing between feelings of having done a good job and having "missed the mark".

> Agnes, Ni/Te (INTJ), company coach in a large organization, felt handicapped for a long time by her feeling of total incompetence. During each session, a tiny voice whispered to her: "What a

loser you are – what you are doing is really stupid! What an imposter!" and she had no confidence whatsoever in her abilities, which were actually very significant. For her, coaching was very painful – even giving her terrible stomach aches – until one day, when she faced up to this Loser part of herself. Instead of trying to eliminate it, she simply named it "Albert", a name which she found appropriately pathetic. Having named this part, she was able to put Albert at a distance. In every session, she mentally seated Albert next to her; if she said or did something pathetic, it wasn't a major problem – it was to be expected of Albert the Loser; but Agnes herself had no trouble picking things up and continuing. Albert was not her! Finally one day, it dawned on her that Albert was the most thoughtful part of her, the one that needed time to create distance and not rush into action, and, in this way, it was an extremely beneficial part.

On the other hand, some coaches may be lacking their own "Albert". It is very useful in deflating an overconfident ego. The feeling of omnipotence, of being able to "work magic" also needs its counterbalance, because without it, the coach soon sees himself as a guru.

A beginning coach said in surprise one day: "With my last client, I just wanted to make 'a quick little adjustment to the inferior function' – and I don't know, it really backfired on me".

Most certainly! And that is for the best, because we do not play with these self-development approaches as if they were a box of tools to be applied from the outside, as if we were a sorcerer's apprentice.

The Savior and the Uncaring

The "Savior" is quite common in the coaching professions; coaches truly have the goal of helping others. A small dose of Savior is definitely useful, but the problem is that, like all the primary Sub-Personalities, it has an annoying tendency to become hegemonic, wanting to save the client at all costs, even against the client's wishes. The Savior really likes Extraverted Feeling coaches; it has a natural alliance with them. But if the coach is identified with the Savior, this can be a form of power, and the client ends up indebted.

It's up to the Savior to apply the famous phrase attributed to Confucius: "When a man is hungry, it is better to teach him to fish than to give him one." But here as well, the Savior can revert to its opposite and blow up: "Leave me in peace and go find your own darn fish!" or "That's your problem!"

The Problem Solver and the Lily of the Field

The Problem Solver is the Sub-Personality that loves giving advice and finding practical solutions, going so far as to do this in the client's stead. It is particularly annoyed by the application of the following principle: "The coach's only goal is to help the client develop the Aware Ego that is appropriate for the current situation". The Problem Solver really wants its client to leave with a solid action plan. That might be useful, but it's not the most important thing. In actuality, if the client achieves an Aware Ego, he will then find the solutions. The problems are his own, and he is qualified to solve them once the coach has mobilized, in a balanced fashion, all the resources he will need, thereby widening the range of choices. Giving in to the temptation of quick fixes is simply ceding to the pressures of daily life and does not create the space needed for the emergence of the Aware Ego.

Coaches who are type Si/Te or Te/Si are most certainly feeling a twinge of annoyance reading these lines. A voice within them is crying out, maybe even quite loudly: "Well, we need results. The company isn't paying for us just to play around – you have to be realistic (efficient, practical, etc.)". This is the right moment to ask oneself whose Operating Ego is feeling irritated and is sliding over to center stage to join the chorus with the employer's Operating Ego.

However, that doesn't mean we should let the opposite pole in turn steal the show and slide into Know-it-All mode – "ya just gotta..., ya just hafta..." or "I could care less!". The fact that it is written in Gospels "*Look at the lilies and how they grow. They don't weave or make their clothing, yet Solomon in all his glory was not dressed as beautifully as they are.*" (Luke 12:27) does not mean that we are exempted from using our weaving loom.

THE VARIOUS STAGES OF COACHING

The coach's role will be noted to take a practical form at different stages of the coaching process, most particularly:

- Analyzing the request.
- Establishing the contract.
- Setting a goal.
- Doing an initial mapping.
- Evaluating.

The type of approach used is left up to the coach. However, it is a relationship of two individuals, and therefore:

- the comments that we are going to make regarding the coach are "reversible" – clients can apply each comment to themselves in a symmetrical fashion.
- in some cases, we will clearly pinpoint a client's position in the light of the Intelligence of Self.

Analyzing the Request

The question "Who is speaking?" now becomes "Who is speaking within whom?"

Several individuals can, in fact, make a request for coaching. The three most common are:

- an interested individual
- a supervisor
- a Human Resources representative.

At times, there is only one person involved, and at others, all three are present. In that case, they may all be speaking with the same voice, or they may express differing opinions. The coach's work will then be to help the various applicants speak to each other in order to determine a shared objective.

In terms of Intelligence of Self, the same question may be asked, and perhaps should be asked, in regard to each of the applicants. Which voice, which Sub-Personality is requesting the coaching? This can be:

- within the supervisor who is suggesting coaching for the subordinate:
    - a Savior racing to help someone who is struggling,
    - a Defeatist, muttering "Whatever..." and just trying to get the problem off his desk, or
    - a Slave Driver or Persecutor[17] blaming everything on its victim.
- within the Human Resources employee/staff member:
    - another Savior.
    - an Experimenter who is curious about new approaches.
    - an Obedient Child working on a self-development program that was imposed on him.
- within the client:
    - a Good Student who wants to please the boss.
    - a Victim seeking a Savior.
    - an Ambitious Person looking for a promotion.
    - a Manipulator who has absolutely no intention of getting involved.

By asking the question in these terms, we are going much further than simply determining the motivation, as it broadens the field of investigation:

- It fits the approach into a group of behaviors, convictions, and beliefs which go beyond the immediate question of coaching. If, for example, the Savior is the reason for the request of one of the individuals involved, we will see behind it a history of rescues – successful or failed – as well as expectations and needs that may be more or less satisfied. This all puts an extra burden on the request

---

[17] The terms "Savior", "Slave Driver" or "Persecutor", "Victim" designate interchangeable roles that three individuals can play in relationship to one another; a "dramatic triangle" is thus formed. See especially *Codependent No More*, Melodie Beatty, Pocket, 2004

for coaching; there is extra signification without there necessarily being any direct connection to the request, and the impact is that we "over-determine".
- It brings us necessarily to ask ourselves about the opposite pole, because for each voice which speaks out in favor of the coaching, there is surely another which doesn't like the idea or that feels some reservations. That voice is saying nothing for the moment. But it will most likely show up eventually. It serves no purpose to provoke it when it is quiet, but don't be surprised when it does speak up.

Let's look at a specific example involving an individual being coached, because if the question "Who is speaking?" can be asked of each of the individuals involved in a request for coaching, it is of significant importance for both the client and the coach.

> Judith, Te/Si (ESTJ), Extraverted Thinking/Introverted Sensing, is a 35-year-old political science graduate. She is a senior-level manager, identified as having very high potential, in an industrial organization where the vast majority of her colleagues and peers are male engineers. Born into very modest circumstances, she has forged a remarkable career, with a reputation for being "as tough as nails". Until the day when, for reasons of a significant restructuring, she is ordered to dismantle the team that she has just spent two years creating.
>
> At this point Judith is shattered. She asks HR for coaching because she can't see any way for her to overcome her difficulties alone. During the first meeting with the coach, she spends most of the time crying, and the rest of the time saying how ashamed she is of crying. She specifies that what saddens her the most is having to break apart the team that she brought together, betraying their trust, and never again being able to exercise the protective role that she had assumed up to that point.

We can hear the two opposite polarities within Judith expressing themselves:

- The request for coaching is openly expressed by the part of her that can't find a way out of her troubles, the part that is a victim of unforeseen, undesirable events.
- This part is speaking out because the strong pole, the Operating Ego has just bumped up against its limits. Her all-powerful "tough as nails", and "protective mother" Selves are no longer appropriate for dealing with the new situation. It's also this part that makes her feel guilty for crying.

This situation, however painful it may be for Judith to experience, can prove to be a remarkable opportunity for progress. If one understands and undertakes the work of challenging the Operating Ego, new options and possibilities will appear. We can predict that the resulting development of the Aware Ego will carry over into other areas. Having thus heard two Sub-Personalities speak out, the coach can express sincere compassion without falling into the trap of playing Savior, because his objective is to permit the Aware Ego to emerge through awareness of the opposite polarities.

Establishing the Contract

Establishing the contract raises a variety of questions: duration, frequency of sessions, location, coaching fee, etc. Our goal here is not to deal with these issues, but rather, by staying true to the approach, to ask the question "Who within the coach is setting up the contract?" Or – who isn't thinking about setting it up!

Different Sub-Personalities may be at work, and among all of them, it is appropriate to have the Aware Ego come forth, as it is the only part suitable to establish the contract. As an example, we will look at two pairs of opposite functions that are particularly involved.

Introverted Sensing – Extraverted Intuiting

For many Extraverted Intuiting coaches of the Extraverted Intuiting type, there is often a risk that they will neglect the concrete details of the contract (fees, payment method, intervention format, detailed program). And for many of their clients, the terms are often perceived as being too vague or too general: a common question is "What will we do exactly?" It is then appropriate for the coach to further integrate the pole that he tends to forget and find the right balance between the concept and the details.

However, it is important not to go to opposite extremes, which could easily be the case for Introverted Sensing types: a coaching contract is not a 20-page document outlining everything that will occur – this would slow down the client's growth and limit the coach's options.

Extraverted Thinking – Introverted Feeling

This pair of opposites is particularly useful in helping the coach set his fees, a question which must be resolved by each coach on an individual basis. This is done not simply by collecting relevant information (local market, type of client, expertise of the coach...) but also by operating from the Aware Ego.

It is often not easy to evaluate oneself at a fair value, or especially to "sell" this price to the client. This difficulty is even greater for the "Feeling" types. For instance, it can be observed, that, given equal qualifications, "Feeling" types are paid 20% less than "Thinking" types.

It will therefore be particularly useful for coaches who are a "Feeling" type to call on their "Thinking" side in order to get the distance necessary, and only then proceed with a more objective self-evaluation and exercise their assertiveness in stating their rates. They can also seek help or coaching on this topic.

In a contrary sense, as well, it may be useful for certain "Thinking" types to demonstrate flexibility and not take shelter behind rate scales or rigid procedures.

This problem is a fundamental one in the field of coaching. It raises the question of self-esteem, of what each person believes he is worth, of what he can bring to the client. It also raises the question of consideration for an individual's circumstances and payment for services offered to those in financial difficulty. Principles are easy to put on paper; putting them into practice demands constant reflection and an ongoing effort to act, in these areas, from the Aware Ego. The time invested here will help avoid pendulum swings in the form of frustration, anger for having been "used" or "had", or feelings of guilt for having been greedy.

Identifying Objectives

We can think of the objectives in terms of "client objectives" and "coach objectives".

The Client's Objectives

The client most often expresses an objective in relation to a specific need: a difficult transition that must be completed, a troubling professional or personal relationship, a tough decision to be made.... As we saw earlier, the first request for coaching comes from the Operating Ego or from one of the Sub-Personalities which form it. The client's objective is, in theory, achieved when the need has been satisfied and the problem resolved.

We say "in theory" as there are two things that arise to complicate the situation:

- One objective often masks another, and once the first goal is reached, a second one appears. This is how a relationship difficulty with a co-worker, which was in fact the initial reason for establishing the coaching sessions, reveals the client's difficulty expressing his feelings. Or how a client's difficulty taking on new job responsibilities leads to a career change.
- As the work progresses, the specific goal turns into a greater objective, that of the development of the Aware Ego. When an Aware Ego begins to emerge, it transforms the global outlook, and it puts all events in a new perspective, and this, as a result, brings forth new objectives. In fact, it undertakes a complete rebuilding of the psyche. From that point, new objectives can appear.

In a "domino effect", this disidentification from one's Operating Ego and the resulting emergence of the Aware Ego echo through all areas of the client's life, not just the area that was initially targeted.

> During her coaching sessions, Judith is easily able to spot her Operating Ego, which resembles Joan of Arc, an armored fighter in a man's world, doggedly following her extremely demanding inner voices with regard to the goal of achieving perfection. The consequences are important for her professional progression, but also, in an unexpected way, for her personal growth: when she becomes pregnant, she observes that her Joan of Arc is intolerant of "the ageless weakness of women" and her morning nausea. Having become aware of this, Judith finds that she is able to go back to bed with a clear conscience and then go to work later in the day, when she can be much more efficient.

The Coach's Objectives

The objective of the coach is to assist the client reach his own goal. The client can only do this if operating from an Aware Ego. And thus, the only objective the coach has is to assist the client develop an Aware Ego appropriate for the current situation. To emphasize this point: the client's objective is their own – it is not the coach's. This means in very real terms that the coach has no input with respect to the content, that he has no right to intervene here. The coach's only job is to assist the client "reclaim" the internal resources that will succeed in balancing the actual, existing resources in order to enable the Aware Ego to emerge. And it is the client who will find the best solution for the current challenge.

This sets a very clear course for the work of the coach. The path may be twisted and difficult to follow, but the goal is always the same: to help the client perceive the opposites in order to let the Aware Ego emerge.

Doing an Initial Mapping

At the beginning of the work, we go through a process of mapping out the individual's ways of functioning. We prefer the term initial "mapping" rather than "diagnosis" which would imply a clinical relationship between the client and the coach.

What is the purpose of this? To help the client identify his modes of operation. To this end, Jungian typology is a particularly useful and efficient instrument, as it:

- deals with the whole of an individual's psychic life – all areas without any distinction made between professional and personal life.
- is based on the fundamental principle of the opposing polarities, and it specifically highlights which of the 8 functions are preferred.
- enables the coach to establish a baseline of the psyche on which he can gradually place, more or less precisely, the adaptation strategies used by the client.
- is non-evaluative: It does not "lock in" a client, rather it gives a client the keys to his self-development.

This assessment of the psyche will continue to evolve over time as the typology expands through identification of dominant and nonintegrated strategies, and through further discoveries related to the nature and characteristics of the Operating Ego.

Evaluating

There are two types of objective to evaluate:

- the objective established initially, the basis for the original contract, and
- the larger objective, which will emerge with the development of the Aware Ego.

We can identify three situations depending on the party concerned: the employer who pays for the coaching, the client, and the coach.

The Employer

Employers will be principally interested in the results compared to the initial objective.

The Client

Who, within the client, will take part in the evaluation? If the coaching went well, it will be, in theory, the Aware Ego. This is the only part which can participate in an evaluation of the two objectives described above. As for the Operating Ego, it can only evaluate in terms of the initial objective – which, in fact, it is nonetheless important to achieve!

The Coach

The coach views the evaluation from two different perspectives:

- As with all moments during coaching, the coach helps the client access the Aware Ego, and
- For himself, the coach takes part in his own evaluation, which has two fundamental criteria:
    - Did he work from the Aware Ego?
    - Was he able to help the client in the process of the emerging Aware Ego?

THE COACHING RELATIONSHIP

The relationship between coach and client is obviously an essential element of the coaching. The relationship wouldn't even exist if there were not a resonance of some form or other between the coach and the client. This means that the emotions that each is going to feel in relation to the other are of paramount importance.

In the framework of therapy we often refer to:

- Transference – a process by which a client undergoing therapy projects onto the psychoanalyst either affection (positive transference) or hostility (negative transference) that was originally felt, especially during childhood, towards another significant person in the environment (mother, father, etc.).
- Counter-transference – all of the coach's unconscious reactions to the individual under analysis and more particularly to the transference by the individual. Counter-transference can also be positive or negative.

These processes make up the essence of the psychoanalytic experience and have been studied in depth.

In the framework of coaching, we believe it is preferable to review the processes of transference and counter-transference differently, paying less attention to what happens within the client in relationship to the coach, and more attention to the relationship between the two principal figures – the coach and the client. And if we apply the principles of Intelligence of Self here, we will be less interested in the relationship between the two individuals, and more interested in the Bonding Pattern that arises between the various Sub-Personalities – the coach's and the client's.

The Positive Bonding Pattern

Generally the relationship begins with a positive Bonding Pattern. If the client hates the coach on sight, or if the coach finds it impossible to empathize with the potential client, there will simply be no start to the coaching relationship. This is the reason why most companies offer a number of coaches for the potential client to choose from:

- either the client receives a list of several coaches that he can get to know,
- or a coach is recommended to the client, with the option of seeing others if the first one does not suit.

Becoming Who You Are with the Intelligence of Self

In a Bonding Pattern, there is almost always a part that is visible right from the start, and another one that is not as easy to identify.

Here the visible part is the assistance that the client is requesting from the coach. As an analyst once said to a client who was explaining at length the very rational reasons for undertaking analysis, and who also admitted to some personal difficulties: "You know, everyone who comes to see me has some kind of problem!" We find then:

1. The client's issue, the reason he is seeing a coach, the part that feels fragile.
2. The coach's expertise: his ability to help the client develop the Aware Ego, the help he can offer.

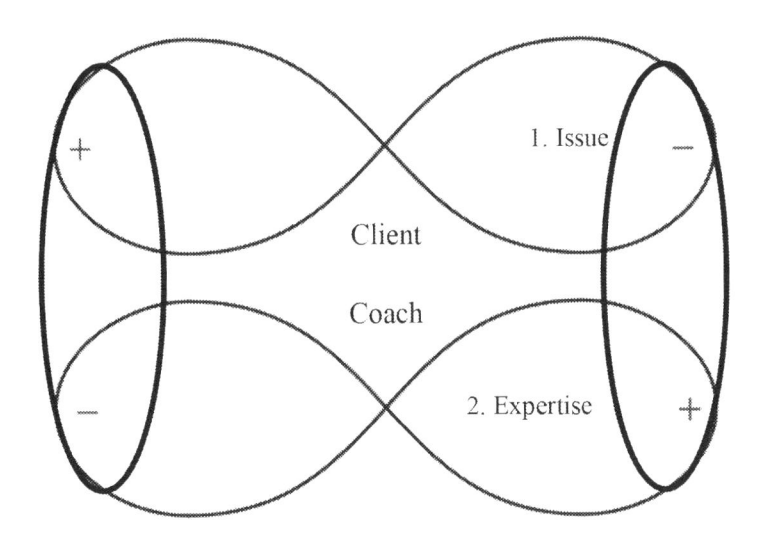

Figure 6.1 – Positive Bonding Pattern Coach – Client

The part that is less immediately visible, but that is just as real, is the way in which the coach needs the client.

Two principal cases can arise.

Bonding Pattern Based on Fee for Service

1. The coach earns a living plying his trade. As does everyone, the coach needs to earn money. The greater this need, the greater the coach's dependence on the client.
2. The client is the payer. His distress is often so great that he is not aware of this power, but it is real. The client supports the coach financially.

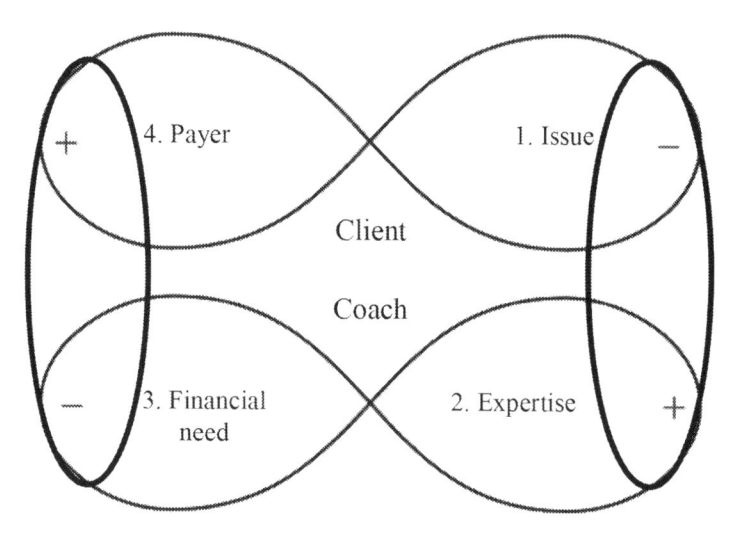

Figure 6.2 – Positive Bonding Pattern Coach – Client Based on Fee for Service

Bonding Pattern Based on Gratification of the Coach

3b. The coach has a need for recognition. There is within a child seeking approval.

4b. The client plays the role of grateful parent: "The services that you have provided are extraordinary. I'll never be able to repay you!"

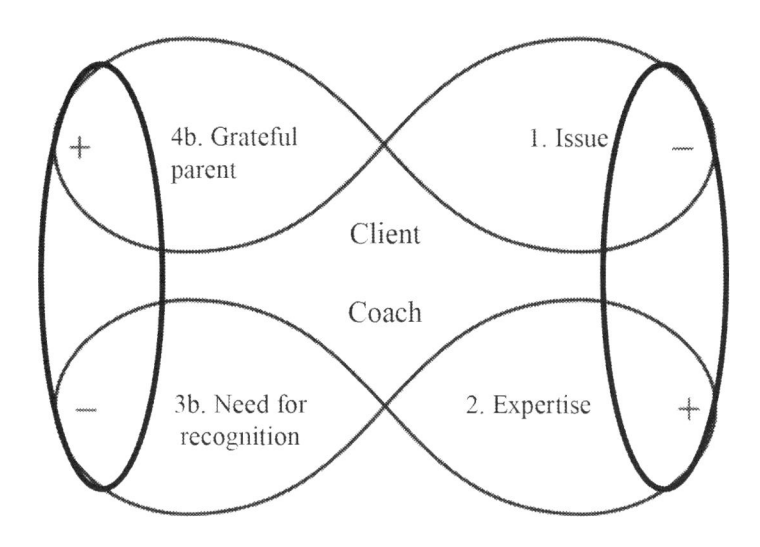

Becoming Who You Are with the Intelligence of Self

```
    4b. Grateful           1. Issue
    parent
              Client
              Coach
    3b. Need for           2. Expertise
    recognition
```

Figure 6.3 – Positive Bonding Pattern Coach – Client Based on Gratification of the Coach

These sample scenarios may take a variety of forms; many others may be created according to the Sub-Personalities at work in both the client and the coach.

The Negative Bonding Pattern

Sooner or later a Bonding Pattern changes from positive to negative. In the current example, there are several causes that can bring about this reversal:

- Deterioration of the relationship over time. Coaching generally is of a briefer duration than therapy so this is rare but still remains possible.
- The coach makes a mistake. It happens – no one is perfect. For example:
    - The coach says something, essentially fair and accurate, but inopportune or awkward.
    - The coach interprets incorrectly, in other words, he gives the client an incorrect explanation.

- The client is faced with a difficulty and tries to escape it; it is in this case much easier to accuse the coach and justify getting out of the relationship. "Give a dog a bad name and hang him!"[18]

So what can happen in this case?

1. The dissatisfied client turns into a judge. He can clearly state the reasons for his dissatisfaction. This is, in relative terms, the easiest outcome, because dialogue can take place. The client can also express dissatisfaction indirectly, by being late to sessions, withholding information, being uncooperative, or even announcing that the coaching is not serving any purpose and quitting.

> Claudine, 45 years old, is a management executive in an industrial company. As she is a type Ne/Fi (ENFP), she is bored in her work and is looking for a new career direction within the company or even elsewhere. Human relationships are her passion: her father is a therapist himself and has had a great influence on her. She is undergoing therapy and wants to explore the professional side of her growth this way.
>
> The first five sessions progress normally: she identifies her type and is able to come to practical conclusions regarding her professional direction; she brings up the Bonding Pattern she has with her husband, who is a very different type. Everything seems to be progressing well when, during the sixth session, she declares that after a great start to the work, she is now feeling like she is floundering; she adds that it's not the first time that this has happened to her. To top it all off, her father, whom she has relied on for all decisions, has just indicated that he no longer wants to "take care of her".
>
> Although the next session is scheduled, Claudine doesn't show up. She calls in to say simply that she no longer has time for the coaching.

---

[18] Molière, *Les Femmes savantes*, Act II, scene 5. "Qui veut noyer son chien, l'accuse de la rage"

2. Depending on the Sub-Personality at work in the positive Bonding Pattern, the coach's reaction may vary. For many, the client's attitude will send them back to a feeling of inadequacy or incompetence. The Loser strikes again. "Does what I'm doing make any sense?" "So what mistake did I make *this time*?" In this last question, it should be noted that the words 'this time' reveal the Sub-Personality at work. The fact that the coach is reflecting on the possibility that a mistake has been made reveals a very sound code of ethical conduct; supervision by a more experienced practitioner is particularly helpful to explore these kinds of issues. But the words 'this time' are too much, as if this situation occurred regularly, as if it wasn't just one error, one specific slip, but rather a fundamental flaw or recurring state of affairs.

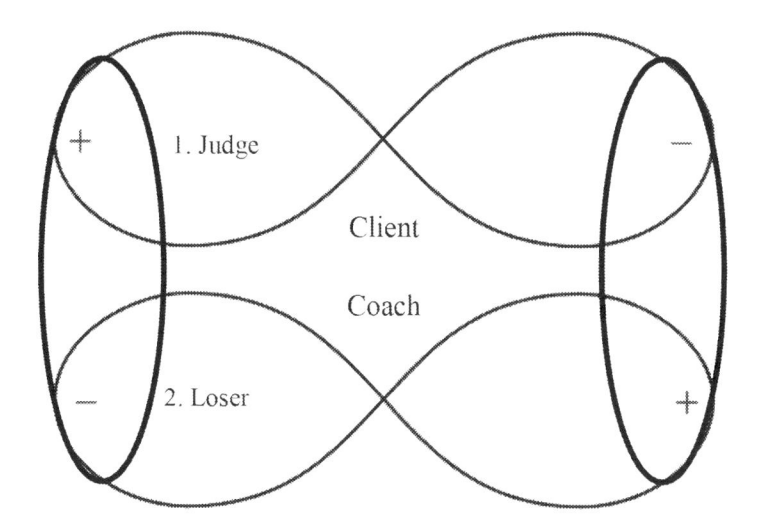

Figure 6.4 – Negative Bonding Pattern Coach – Client

Of course the Bonding Pattern doesn't end there – there is a symmetrical relationship which will play out. The possibilities are virtually endless!

3. To compensate for the feeling of being "a loser" the coach can use his expertise in a punitive manner, "getting up on his high horse!"

> A coach said to a client, who had just expressed very strong criticism: "I have noticed that it is always the clients we offer reduced rates to who are the most demanding". Ouch!

Without going that far, the coach can easily "punish" the client by interpreting criticism as resistance. This can, of course, truly be the case, but the term 'resistance' is quite often a label which puts the responsibility for the blockage on the client and which enables the coach to evade any feeling of uneasiness.

4. The last step of the Bonding Pattern: the client obviously feels rejected in one way or another. He is blamed for having expressed himself and is not a "good" client.

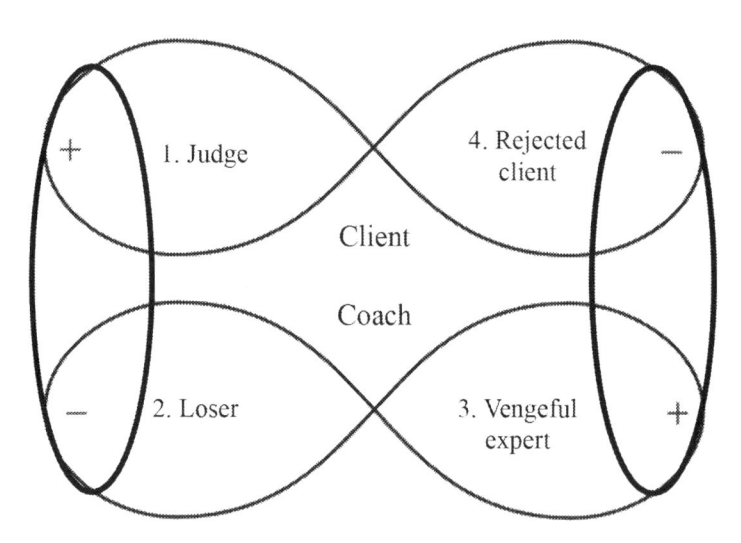

Figure 6.5 – Possible Development of Negative Bonding Pattern Coach – Client

The Relationship of Aware Ego (Coach) to Aware Ego (Client)

In theory and in an ideal world, the Bonding Pattern described above would never progress to its conclusion. This is because, in fact, it is the coach's role to maintain his Aware Ego in order to understand what is playing out within the client and help his Aware Ego emerge. In actual practice, everyone does their best!

So how can the coach establish a relationship of Aware Ego to Aware Ego? There are three answers.

The Coach's Aware Ego

The first answer may appear somewhat obvious: the coach must constantly be on alert regarding his own Aware Ego process. This is exactly why the coach must pursue his own self-development and "meet" as many Sub-Personalities as possible, so as not to be surprised by any that do show up during the coaching sessions.

Awareness of the Bonding Patterns

Secondly, the coach must be aware of the positive Bonding Pattern which is unavoidably established between the client and the coach. This doesn't mean that the coach shares this knowledge with the client. In the vast majority of cases, it would be completely out of place. But it means the coach must be very aware of the cornerstones of the Bonding Pattern – exactly what the client wants from the coach, and how in particular the relationship is gratifying to the coach.

The analysis of the Bonding Pattern must be done systematically by the coach for his own purposes, either alone, or with the participation of the coach's supervisor. The help of a supervisor becomes an ethical obligation if at any time the coach feels that the Bonding Pattern may intensify (either due to attraction or repulsion). This will help avoid sliding too quickly or deeply into a negative Bonding Pattern and will enable maintaining the relationship at the level of the Aware Ego, at least for the coach.

Discussion with the Client?

As the Bonding Pattern turns from a positive to a negative pattern, the coach must be doubly cautious to maintain his Aware Ego. He must be very clear about the vulnerable part within himself that is affected by the client's criticism and about the part which could, if the coach does nothing, move into a counter-attack posture. Once again, this work is normally done under supervision. But what should be done if the client broaches this topic in some way?

Unlike some forms of therapy, where transference is the topic of the work, it appears to us unnecessary to take up the issue of the Bonding Pattern with the client. It might be useful in some cases; there is no absolute rule in this area. But within the framework of Intelligence of Self, there is another manner to proceed – it is easier and just as effective.

When the client expresses disapproval or dissatisfaction in a more or less direct manner, it is very useful for the coach to ask this dissatisfied part to express itself, making use of the technique of physical movement to another location, just as would be done with any Sub-Personality. Here, for example, is what the coach could say to a client who reproaches the coach for making a hurtful remark.

> I see that what I just said to you was hurtful for you. It certainly was not my intention to do that, but it's clear that there is a part in you that is reacting strongly to what I said. I would like to understand what fault this voice is finding in the coach, and I would be happy to hear it speak about this. Could you change seats in order to let it speak?

Notice the double distancing that the coach has effected:

- With regard to the client: there is a criticizing voice within the client. It is right for it to express itself, but it is not the client's whole self. Giving it a voice legitimizes it and detaches the client from it all at once.
- With regard to the coach himself: the criticism is not viewed as directed toward the entire person, but only to the "coach" part. By doing this, the coach can continue in his role, because he is not reduced to it. He can continue to be himself.

In short, the attention that the coach brings to his own process of the Aware Ego is the driving force which enables the client to bring forth his own Aware Ego. This is exactly the reason we say that the coach himself is the tool of the coaching process, and that his own personal development is a professional obligation.

Ethical Considerations

There were two objectives in this chapter:

- Highlighting the impact that the process of Intelligence of Self has on coaching, and
- Using this example to draw conclusions which apply in other fields.

What then are the lessons that we can take away from this?

- Whatever the context may be, the process can be summarized as "enabling the emergence of the Aware Ego".
- The Aware Ego cannot come into existence until each pole has expressed itself freely.
- The Aware Ego is not a state. It is never acquired. It is a permanent path on the ridgeline between two peaks, the path of a tightrope walker on a wire, constantly correcting the tiny imbalances that could topple him to one side or the other.
- It is useful, sometimes even essential, especially at the most difficult times, to call on external support: this is the role of the coach for the client, and the role of the supervisor for the coach.
- As soon as we find ourselves in a relationship, there are no longer simply two people who are communicating and sharing, but rather two families of individuals, with all the different Bonding Patterns that this may entail. When two tightrope walkers set out to meet in the middle, the vibrations and movements of the wire are much more significant.

> *In summary*
>
> So the coach can be this guide along the path to the Aware Ego, provided he pursues his own work. If consideration is given to each particular situation, the questions the coach asks himself at various stages of the process can be carried over into other professional activities and to his personal life.
>
> There are some appropriate tools which can be used to answer these questions and facilitate the access to the Aware Ego. This is the topic of the following chapter.

7

FIVE TECHNIQUES TO HELP YOU ALONG THE PATH

TO HELP YOU ALONG THE PATH, there are several methods that we can use. Here are five which seem particularly useful and effective, to our way of thinking.

The first two methods, Voice Dialogue and Personality Types, require the help of a facilitator, at least at the beginning.

The other three can be practised without help, although working with a facilitator or a group generally leads to better results.

VOICE DIALOGUE

The Method

The Voice Dialogue approach was formulated by two American therapists, Hal and Sidra Stone. The name Voice Dialogue currently has two different meanings.

- Generally, it refers to the totality of the approach and the principles which underpin it. In this sense, this entire book was largely inspired by the Voice Dialogue approach.
- Specifically, it refers to the distinct method that engages the Voice Dialogue principles in the framework of a working session held between client and coach.

We will give a general overview in this section.

The principal notion behind the method is to encourage disidentification from the Auto-Pilot and the integration of the opposite pole by inviting both these parts in turn to move to different locations in the room. In practical terms:

- The client faces the coach; this position, the central seat, is an anchor point. The client sits here at the start and end of each session, and returns here in between each of the different Sub-Personalities. This is the location of the Aware Ego that is in the process of developing. Although absent at the start, if all goes well, it will gradually emerge and take form.
- When a Sub-Personality appears, the coach invites the client to move to another location so it can speak freely. At that point:
  - the coach undertakes a true dialogue with the Sub-Personality by matching and mirroring its tone and energy.
    - The "I" doing the speaking is identified with the Sub-Personality, not with the client, and
    - the coach and the client both refer to the "central" person (the client) in the third person ("he/she").
- When the Sub-Personality has finished speaking, the client returns to the central seat:
  - The "I" that speaks is again the client himself,
  - The coach and client then use the third-person ("he/she") to talk about the Sub-Personality that just spoke.

For the client, learning this verbal and physical "gymnastic routine" takes place quite rapidly in the course of one session. However, underneath its apparent simplicity, the method requires extensive skill and experience on the part of the coach. Let us emphasize the key points:

- The goal of the session is the emergence of the Aware Ego, capable of regulating the Sub-Personalities.
- The impact of a session is not, therefore, measured by the number of Sub-Personalities that appear, but in the quality of the Aware Ego that has been able to emerge.
- The Sub-Personalities never speak to one another, which would simply reproduce what happens typically in the absence of an Aware Ego.

- Each Sub-Personality is invited to express itself freely, completely, and without restraint; only when it has exhausted all it has to say (which does not necessarily happen within one session) will it be able to make space for the opposite pole.
- The coach makes absolutely no evaluation and expresses no judgments about what a Sub-Personality might say; he doesn't contradict it – rather he encourages it to speak its piece fully. Everything shared and every Part sharing is accepted and loved unconditionally.
- As a result, any evaluative language is out of place; positive aspects of a Sub-Personality are not even mentioned, as they would imply other negative aspects. Sub-Personalities are neither positive or negative; everything depends on what the Aware Ego makes of them.

The emergence of the Aware Ego is somewhat like the installation of a mixing valve for a water tap. If we only have warm water to do laundry, it is not ideal: the water will be too cool to wash filthy kitchen rags and too warm for fine silk garments. Both taps are needed – very hot and very cold – and the mixing valve makes it possible to adjust the water to get the desired temperature. In the same way, we don't want to dilute the Sub-Personalities – the stronger they remain, the greater our psychic energy, and the more effective the Aware Ego, our mixing valve, will obviously have to be!

The Plaster Virgin and the Young Girl

This is an example of a Voice Dialogue session.

Helen is a slim, dark-haired woman about 50 years old. Shrewd eyes peer from behind small glasses. A social worker, divorced for two years, she feels torn between the serious side of her life and a desire to laugh and enjoy herself.

Coach – "So you have just mentioned two opposite desires: a very serious part that guides you in your professional and marital life and now a lighter, fun-loving part. Perhaps we could hear from the part that you have known the longest."

Helen gets up, looks around the room carefully and goes to stand behind the coach, near the fireplace, hidden behind a curtain.

Coach – "Hello. Helen told me that you are very serious. I can also see that you are rather unobtrusive as well. What is important about this "hidden" posture you have taken? How does it keep Helen safe?"

Helen from behind the curtain – "I like to observe without being seen. I'm very careful and before speaking or showing myself, I like to know where I'm going to land. I make sure the ground is solid."

Coach – "Because you need to be careful...?"

Shy – "Oh yes. Helen learned this the hard way. When she was quite little, in first grade, she was very playful, and a joker, even a bit of a rebel. But that didn't go over well at school, and I had to intervene."

Coach – "And how did you do that?"

Shy – "Just like now."

Coach – "You mean...."

Shy – "Well, I'm like a white plaster statue of the Virgin Mary. You know the type – you see them in the alcoves in churches. They are very stable, like me; there is no way they will fall. Obviously, I can't move, but on the other hand, I can see everything."

Coach – "How do you do that?"

Becoming Who You Are with the Intelligence of Self

Shy – "I watch things very closely – my eyes are constantly moving. As a result, I see things that are far away, that I would really like to see close up, but I can't move. It's a bit annoying."

Helen remains in her alcove without speaking for a moment, then she returns to the central seat.

Coach – "Yes...."

Helen – "I'm a bit tired of being like that. It's very reassuring, but I feel like a prisoner. At the end of the day, it's not much fun."

Coach – "Maybe we could hear from the fun part?"

Helen gets up again, and this time, she goes to the window. She gives a big smile.

Fun – "Wow! It feels like I'm 6 years old again, when Helen was a child. I feel like doing fun things and taking risks."

Coach – "Are you thinking about anything in particular?"

Fun – "Yes, I've been asked to go facilitate some seminars in Québec. I really want to go. Up north, they aren't as tied down as we are. And I've always dreamed of adventure. You know, the log cabin in Canada, Huskies pulling the sled, all that really has a pull on me."

Coach – "And what do you think of it all?"

Fun – "It's strange – I can see myself with rainbow-colored clothing, and a kite resting on my head. And I would meet lots of new people."

Coach – "Is there something you would like to say to Helen?"

Fun – "Oh yes – short and sweet: 'Just do it!' girl!"

Helen returns to the central seat laughing. From this, she draws two conclusions:

- I won't scrap the plaster Virgin – she's actually not all that bad. I will put her in an alcove, paint her blue, so she'll be a bit more interesting, and give her violets. Like I'm venerating a relic from the past.
- And I'm going to let my little girl live it up a bit more. I don't know if I'll leave tomorrow morning for Québec – I'll have to think about that – but I'm going to start by adding a little more imagination in my life.

PERSONALITY TYPES

Knowing our Personality Type enables us to identify:

- Our ways of functioning – the modes we favor, and the ones we tend to forget.
- Our comfort zones, where the Auto-Pilot sets up spontaneously, and the zones requiring more effort.
- The possible path toward growth and development, and the different stages.

Once we know our Personality Type, we can also "map out" the different Sub-Personalities that are part of our makeup, as we saw earlier with the function cross.

Finally, knowing our Personality Type enables us to recognize how complementary the differences are, and to modify our strategies for adapting to different environments according to our psychic preferences.

Everyone can acquire a certain understanding of their type, as we will see in the next chapter. However, it is very easy to deceive ourselves in this area. This is why a good personality type questionnaire can be very helpful. There are several in existence. We have developed the CCTI[19]

---

[19] CCTI is a registered trademark of Osiris Conseil

(Cauvin-Cailloux Type Indicator) which has two major characteristics: it is easy to use and very efficient[20].

ACTIVE IMAGINATION

Active imagination can be understood to have two different meanings. In general, it consists of using the imagination in an alert state to make contact with the different parts of ourselves. In this sense, all of the approaches we propose in this section fall under active imagination.

In a more restricted sense, active imagination consists of letting the different Parts which make up the Self speak out and facilitating a dialogue between our Aware Ego and the Auto-Pilot or a Sub-Personality. This is done most often as a written dialogue, and here is an example to start.

Robert's Auto-Pilot

Robert, Ni/Te (INTJ), Introverted Intuiting/Extraverted Thinking, wrote a text describing his process of disidentification from his Operating Ego (or Primary Self) and the subsequent reactions.

The different fonts will help identify who is speaking:

- Robert in the Aware Ego Process
- *The Operating Ego or Auto-Pilot*
- A Part or Sub-Personality of Robert's, previously unknown to him

I was enjoying the sun in my backyard when suddenly I heard an authoritarian voice with a steely tone:

- *"What the hell are you doing loafing around? You got nothing better to do? Nothing useful you could work on?"*
- "Hmmm, what…? Who is that? What's going on?"
- *"What do you mean 'Who is that?' Like you don't know me! I've been in your life for the last 65 years. It is true that I'm pretty quiet. Well, quiet, you know – I don't like the spotlight, but I like to take charge."*

---

[20] Interested readers will find our contact information at the end of this book

- "But what do you take charge of?"
- *"You're a damn fool! You, of course. You are the only thing I'm interested in. When you learned to read with your Mom before first grade, that was me. When you were 8 years old and you read your first "Biggles" book in one sitting, that was me. When you got good grades at school, that was me. By the way, you know you could have done better. A little more work and you could have gotten into a major scientific university like your buddy François who got into MIT, the lucky sod."*
- "Yeah, but I wasn't as good at math."
- *"Right, that's true, but you've got to admit that I made you catch up afterward. Three degrees all at the same time, then three jobs all at once – now that was hard work. I was almost proud of you. Not totally, because you can always do better, but, I guess I have to admit that it was pretty darn good."*
- "So what got into you to make me do all that? Now that I think about it, I feel like I didn't have much fun."
- *"Have fun...! Fun...! I'll show you fun! You think life is about having fun? There are higher vocations kiddo, and when you are called, you have to take up the challenge. That's a man's role: to exceed his limits. 'Ad augusta per angusta!'"*
- "Excuse me?"
- *"Oh, so now on top of it all, you've forgotten your Latin, whereas your Dad, when he was 40, could still read Tacitus 'aperto libro' – sorry – open book. You dummy: 'Ad augusta per angusta' is the motto of Jean de la Croix, which Victor Hugo restated in Hernani. It means 'Toward the summits, through narrow paths'."*
- "The extent of your learning impresses me. If that was the goal, you win!"
- *"It's not about impressing anyone – you clearly don't get it. The goal is to keep pushing onward, always coming up with new ideas and putting them into practice. It's a race against yourself, not against anyone else."*
- "Oh, I get it. It's like the joke between Marius and Olive[†] about seeing who could go the fastest."

  "You know", said Olive, "I go so fast that the milestones look like a solid blur along the shoulder."

  "Oh yeah?", said Marius, "I go so fast that I have to honk the horn so I can get by myself."

- "Very funny... really. Do you actually think you'd be where you are now if I hadn't gotten involved?"
- "No, obviously, but I would be somewhere else. I'm curious to know why you came into my life, why it was you that took over the controls instead of someone different, you know, maybe some happy-go-lucky guy, or a wild partier, or a real dunce."
- "Well, you've got me there – that's a bit beyond my competency; I am what I am and that's all there is to it. But, well, now that I think about it, I guess there are two ways to see things. First off, you had some natural qualities that suited me well: you're no dummy, you think about things in depth, and you're organized and methodical. And you get that from your family. Your Dad, who knew his Latin so well, was just a hard-working little orphan who made his way along in life by being so competitive. Your Mom had intellectual qualities that were hidden because in her family, sending girls to university just wasn't done. So that's where I got my start. When I saw you combine all that, there obviously wasn't much need for a lounge chair!"
- "Yeah, I can see that now, but why did you take up so much space over the years?"
- "Well you don't fix something that isn't broken! The better things went, the more I did. Success breeds success. At times, I was like Shiva[†] with 100 arms. It was really enjoyable to see things progress, see plans rise out of the ground or take shape from the ideas and plans I dreamed up."
- "And you never thought of doing things differently?"
- "Differently? What do you mean, differently? Do you want to become one of those little loafers, one of those parasites that suck the system dry, with their employment benefits and cheating on their taxes? Do you actually regret not being some Average Joe with a beer belly? Or would you rather belong to the club of the Know-it-Alls: "Ya just gotta, ya just hafta", those little buggers who always have lots of ideas...for everyone else, but who never actually do anything?"
- "Whoa! I can see you are getting angry."
- "Damn right, I'm angry. It just leaves me speechless. It's just too easy to do sweet nothing and lecture others. It exasperates me that these people can spout empty talk all day, blowing their own horns with nothing to show for it – they are just armchair geniuses who have never touched a shovel handle in their life; they've never

worked at their keyboard until they drop from exhaustion. And if you keep on like that, I'll be pissed at you. Who do you think you are criticizing me after everything I've done for you? Where would you be without me? You want to be mean, well I'll just tell you point blank, you're nothing without me!"

- "I didn't mean to make you angry. I was just wondering what else there is to me when you're not around."
- *"Well I just told you the answer to that – nothing!"*
- "I don't mean to hurt you after everything that you've done for me, but if I'm talking to you, and you're answering back, it means that you're not me, at least, not all of me."
- *"Don't you think your logic is just a little complicated? That's all just a bit too much psycho-babble for me and anyway, excuse me, I've got better things to do with my time."*
- "Hey wait, don't go. I find this conversation absolutely fascinating. You know, I just want to get to know you better. Up to now, I thought you and I were one and the same person. Now I can see that that's not exactly true. So I'd like to know who I am."
- *"You're me!"*
- "I'm not so sure about that any more. Because since we met, I feel like we are different. Besides, I feel like giving you a name, so we don't get mixed up."
- *"Oh yeah? And so what will it be?"*
- "I think that you're my Primary Self."
- *"Oh yeah, sure, call me a primate – insult me – how's that for gratitude after all the degrees I got you!"*
- "But you are willfully misunderstanding me! Primary like 'first', not like 'primate'. It means that you were the first to arrive, that you took the first spot."
- *"Well that's better. So what is your name going to be?"*
- "The Aware Ego."
- *"It just keeps on getting better! What an insult – you make me sound unconscious!"*
- "You're just so touchy! I didn't say that you are unconscious, but that I am conscious of both you and me, whereas you are only conscious of yourself, and that means I'm more aware than you, don't you think?

Becoming Who You Are with the Intelligence of Self

- "I'm just not used to this kind of reasoning. So you think that there is more to you than just you and me?"
- "I'm not sure exactly what there is, but I'm pretty sure that there's more than just you."
- "Hang on, I'm a bit afraid now. What is all this nonsense? What do you mean? I'm not enough for you, is that it? You've found someone else?"
- "Don't get upset, but yes, I think there are other people in me, and I would like to make some space for them."
- "So that's how you reward decades of good and loyal service! You fire me like a dirty bum. I did everything I could for you, and now that you've heard the voice of the sirens, you dump me. You disgust me – it feels like this is some multinational company where they throw out the old lemons once they've been squeezed. That's sure not the lesson I taught you. I see that you've got someone else in your life. Those aren't the values I taught you."

  "O anger! O despair! O age my enemy!
  Have I lived simply to know this infamy!"[21]

- "I can see that this hurts you, but I think we will both end up winning if you aren't the only one in me."
- "Oh, I get it! Don't bother with the sob story. You want me to get lost. Nothing left but to go off and die. Sure, I can do that for you, but really, I never would have thought we'd get to this point."

The Primary Self goes off behind a tree and starts crying, first in loud sobs, then with tears streaming down his face, then like a barrel, slowly emptying itself, dripping interminably.... The Aware Ego waits patiently, kindly. He goes over and offers a Kleenex.

- "How are you doing?"
- "Not great. I'm really sad, really empty. I feel like you don't love me anymore."
- "But of course I love you. I'm even very grateful for everything you've done for me. Enormously grateful and I'm very proud of you. And I'm still really counting on your help in the future. But I would like it to be when I ask you, and not all the time, each time there is something to be done."

---

[21] Pierre Corneille – Le Cid Acte I scène 4

- *"So I'm not out the door?"*
- "What an imagination! Besides, I know you – even if I wanted to get rid of you, it would be impossible."

The Primary Self makes a face and opens its mouth to speak.

- "No, no, wait, don't get angry. I didn't mean to say that I'm only keeping you because there's no other choice. You are a part of me, and I don't want to amputate you. I would just like you not to take up all the space."
- *"It will be hard after so many years reigning alone, but I'd like to give it a try."*
- "Good. And if that's the case...."

The unknown Sub-Personality comes into view.

- "So hey there, guys, I've been trying to get a word in for a while – thanks for finally taking a break!"
- "You're welcome. It's a pleasure to meet you."
- "I hope so, because I know how to do a lot of stuff too, but you've just never asked me to do anything. You only cared about the other guy."
- "I'm sorry about that, but I'm hoping to make up for lost time."
- *"There you go, that's exactly what I was getting at – you're going to dump me!"*
- "Listen, I understand your reaction, but if you keep interrupting all the time, we won't get anywhere. I promise you that you'll get a chance to talk again. But in the meantime, can you just be quiet for five minutes?"
- *"Grrr...."*
- To the unknown Sub-Personality: "You were saying?"
- "Don't go believing what the other is saying about me. He wants me to look like a good-for-nothing or an idiot. That's not the case at all. Do you know how to enjoy a sunset without having finished all your emails? Do you know how to play with your granddaughters with no other expectation than the pleasure of being with them? Do you know

```
          how to tell stories without turning them into a
          teaching tool? Do you know how to watch a flower
          grow without getting impatient? Do you know how
          to watch the light playing on the clouds? Do you
          know how to just be there, to simply be?
```
- "No, not really. I've heard about all that, but I didn't know that it was you showing up in my life."
- *"I have a full bibliography available for you on the subject."*
- "That's very nice, thank you, but can you just wait a bit longer, please."
- ```
  "Bibliographies aren't really my forte, but I can
  sure show you how to live the experience fully,
  how to be...."
  ```
- "Thank you."
- To the Primary Self: "So are you doing OK with this?"
- *"Well if you read the books that I suggest so you understand what you're doing, things will be just fine!"*
- "Thanks to both of you. I'm looking forward to see where this collaborative effort will lead us!"

Now It's Your Turn!

First Step: Identify the Auto-Pilot (Primary Self/Operating Ego)

The Operating Ego is not easily identified because at first, it takes itself for the entire person. It occupies all the space. The real pilot isn't in the plane yet. This is precisely the reason that the help of a coach is of great benefit. But there is nothing preventing us from walking part of the trail on our own. Here are some suggestions and questions:

- Discover your psychological type, and to do this, rely on a qualified practitioner or read one of our books noted in the bibliography. Your Operating Ego is most likely linked, at least in part, to your psychological type and your preferred functions.
- Imagine the praise and commendations that might be directed your way during an awards ceremony (or any ceremony).
  ```

- How do you typically describe yourself? "I always look out for others", "I'm honest", "I'm a hard worker", "I'm not this...or that...", etc. This way of speaking – "I'm X or Y..." is, in general, our Operating Ego; the Aware Ego embraces the opposites, and it is not identified with either "X" or "Y".
- What do others typically say about you? In what areas, for what services do others seek you out?
- What is, or was, your nickname?

Second Step: Have a Conversation with Your Auto-Pilot

No matter what the content of this conversation might be, it is aimed at detaching you from your Auto-Pilot to enable the emergence of the Aware Ego. A few things to note:

- The conversation therefore takes place between the Aware Ego and the Auto-Pilot. It is important not to digress and to be attentive to what you are writing. The Aware Ego is attempting to understand the Auto-Pilot; it is conducting an interview to shed some light on the Operating Ego and to create some distance from it.
- Use the method which suits you the best – use a pen or a keyboard. In either case, show the transition from one voice to the other – make it visual – by changing the appearance of the font (color, bold, italics, etc.).

Third Step: Let the Opposite Pole Speak

- Give the Operating Ego all the time it needs to express everything it wants to say.
- When the opposite pole is ready to speak, open the discussion following the same rules.
- Always end with the Aware Ego, which can really only come forward when the two opposites have clearly distinguished themselves. The Aware Ego can be heard at that point as a third voice (a third way) with regard to the initial situation.

TAKING BACK PROJECTIONS

Projections are positive or negative feelings felt toward another in a disproportionate degree, because we attribute to the other the things we do not or cannot see in ourselves.

Anne and Lucy

Anne is in her forties. She is an HR professional who is taking a personal development seminar comprised of several modules. She is serious, responsible, well known in her field. Another group participant, Lucy, is the manager of a consulting firm; she is slightly younger, always well dressed, and always concerned for her own comforts, going to all ends to achieve this.

Anne's growing irritation with Lucy was not apparent at all, until one day when Lucy was absent. Suddenly abandoning her usual reserved manner, Anne declared aloud:

> Well good riddance! She's always a pain in the butt, imposing her every whim on us – "Oh please, a cushion, a glass of water..." – Get serious! She's like the queen bee. I'm surprised she doesn't have us all running around serving her and changing the seminar to suit her needs. Who does she think she is – some princess that we should all be at her beck and call, satisfying her slightest desires!"

Anne goes on in this fashion, imitating Lucy with uncanny accuracy. After a few moments of reflection, she realizes what has just happened.

- Lucy knows how to do what Anne cannot permit herself to do: express her own desires. Her upbringing and her career have taught her to not ask: she is to listen, to remain in the background, to think first of others. The fact that another person might so casually be able to do something she doesn't know how to do hits her in a very sensitive area that is completely unknown to her.
- Their psychological types are almost completely opposite:
    - Anne is an Ni/Fe (INFJ); she has Introverted Intuiting as the dominant function and Extraverted Sensing as the inferior function. She is therefore much more at ease in the

world of concepts and writing than in the material world. Moreover, her Extraverted Feeling as auxiliary pushes her into serving others. Everything is in place to make her neglect her own needs.
- Lucy is an Se/Ti (ESTP). She thus has Anne's inferior function as her own dominant function – Extraverted Sensing makes her very much at ease in the real world, and she has a strong ability to modify the external world according to her needs. Additionally, her Introverted Thinking as auxiliary pushes her to step back and prioritize easily. This means she has no difficulty identifying what would make her happy and how to get it.

With her understanding of what has happened, Anne's life changes dramatically. Not only does she stop being irritated by Lucy's words and deeds, but she also begins, in turn, to discover and express her own needs and then satisfy them. This brings about considerable improvement in her enjoyment of life and does not in the least impact her professional attitude.

Adriana and Renata

Adriana (Fi/Ne, INFP) and Renata (Fe/Si, ESFJ) are two young blonds, both attractive and intelligent. When they begin to work together, Renata very quickly experiences negative feelings toward Adriana.

In Renata's family, appearances are always of the utmost importance. An attractive appearance is a calling card that guarantees acceptance by the Other. It is necessary to care for one's appearance, going as far as orthodontic procedures and beauty treatments. The relationship with the other person is just as important; "being pretty" is not sufficient – she must also be nice in order to be accepted. This is absolutely essential, and it suits Renata, as she is an Extraverted Feeling type, which makes it easy for her to relate to others.

Renata views Adriana as dangerous, because:

- she sees Adriana as prettier than herself, seemingly without effort, and
- she judges her to be very secretive and reserved; even if Adriana is stunning in Renata's eyes, she is nonetheless very elusive.

Renata is immediately irritated by Adriana; she finds her seductive and manipulative. Her silences are weighty. What might she be thinking under that beautiful hairdo?

In a similar fashion, Adriana, who is an Introverted Feeling type, has difficulty expressing her feelings. She could do this, if only Renata would give her a bit of time. But no, she is constantly intervening in such a categorical fashion; everything is always black and white. Adriana finds her to be invasive, sure of herself to the point of arrogance, with her cutting tone of voice and her assurance.

In the course of a long exchange facilitated by a coach, Adriana and Renata are able to express what they are each feeling with respect to the other, and they arrive at an understanding of how they push each other's buttons.

They can then each begin to take back their judgments:

- Renata understands that Adriana's silences are not due to any "deviousness" but rather that she needs time to understand and express the depths of what she is feeling within.
- Adriana realizes that Renata is not trying to take control but that she willingly communicates her values and feelings with the best intentions in the world, even if this doesn't always occur at the most opportune times.

They can then integrate within themselves the aspects that were so irritating in the other:

- Renata: "I can think to myself without necessarily having to share my thoughts! I can be accepted, even if I am not always acting in an extraverted way, and I might have an easier time relating to Introverted Feeling types if I were a bit quieter, a bit less abrupt."

- Adriana: "I realize now that I can upset or even hurt some people by my silences! The others are more interested by what's going on in me than I ever thought! I can try to share my thoughts a bit more, even if things are not totally clear in my head yet."

Now It's Your Turn!

Understanding why some people upset us and integrating within ourselves what they know how to do and we don't – these are some of the best self-development techniques that exist. In fact, we should raise a statue to anyone who really irritates us, because these individuals are our teachers. For this reason, completing the following exercise is highly instructive[22]:

- Make a list of those individuals who bother you.
- Choose the number one ranked individual on the list.
- Write down what bothers you about this person, and why you are critical of him.
- Find the quality behind the apparent flaw. This is the most difficult part: it is so difficult not to judge the other that the purported "positive" quality that we select is usually only another negative aspect in disguise. If someone irritates me because I find him manipulative, I will probably start by trying to formulate the positive side as being something like this: "Yes, if I knew how to show myself off like he does, I would have better success." This isn't really the wording of a positive quality, which, in fact, would be much more like: "This person knows how to relate to others and to have an easy-going, friendly contact with them." Here are some examples of how we can possibly reframe a negative quality into a positive one:
    - Bossy = Assertive
    - Selfish = Skilled in self-care
    - Braggart = Aware of own self-worth

---

[22] This exercise is based on J'aime ona Pangaïa's book which is cited in the bibliography.

- Withdrawn = Capable of introspective reflection
- "Special" = Able to hold self in high esteem
- Identify the lack within us that makes us irritable when we consider the other. Following up on the previous example, this could be shyness, a lack of social skills, a lack of spontaneity in expressing one's feelings.
- Finally, ask the question: "If I were to take an extremely tiny dose of that quality that irritates me so much in the other person, what could I do that I can't do currently, or what could I do better than I do now?"

BY THE LIGHT OF OUR DREAMS

If "dreams are the royal road to our unconscious"[23] and if "every unexamined dream is like an unread letter", what a shame to miss this opportunity!

Here are two examples, followed by some suggestions.

Christine's Cats

Christine's type is Fe/Ni (ENFJ), Extraverted Feeling as dominant function and Introverted Intuiting as auxiliary function. The opposite poles are thus Extraverted Sensing (as tertiary function) and Introverted Thinking (as inferior). Christine is starting out on a professional path after having spent the first half of her life as a wife and stay-at-home Mom. She is energetic, active, generous, and she likes to take matters into her own hands. At the start of her self-development work, she is strongly identified with her values. Here is her dream:

Christine states that this dream had a very strong impact on her. For her, there are clearly two parts with very different emotions:

- The first part, the "enraged cat" which brings out fear, terror, and the anguish of being attacked repeatedly, as if by a devil that could appear at any moment.

---

[23] Both quotations are attributed to Sigmund Freud[†]

- The second part, in front of the kittens and their mother, which brings out feelings of emotion, warmth, softness, recognition, and tenderness.

Beyond the specific meanings that Christine was able to draw for her personal life, this dream is rich in lessons:

- Seen by the Primary Self, the inferior function looks like a dangerous animal: *"I'm holding an enraged cat...."*.

The primary Sub-Personality exacerbates the problem by closing the doors. For as long as the doors remain locked, the shadow keeps returning to attack, each time more powerfully.

- The cat Christine fears in her dream expresses values that are different from the values of Christine's Primary Self: liberty, independence, tranquility. But these values are not integrated; they are still "*in the sideboard*".
- To open the sideboard, masculine intervention is required: *"Then a man comes in to tell me that... I should go into the next room"*. The inferior function is often projected onto a person of the opposite sex, and that is what happens here. Additionally, it is Introverted Thinking, a function that is culturally masculine and thus close to the animus.
- In fact, when Christine opens the door of the sideboard, or in other words, when she separates from her dominant Sub-Personality, it's no longer an enraged cat, but instead five kittens that appear. The inferior function was only a monster because it was rejected. As soon as Christine opens the door, it is the gentle side of the inferior function that appears.
- These are kittens, signifying that this part is at the beginning of its existence; it is still in its infancy. But now it is accessible without any risk of scratches or claw marks.

- The kittens are inside the sideboard, expressing the introverted side of this function.
- The tertiary function is, however, projected onto a person of the same sex: here, the mother cat represents an instinctive drive (Se) in direct contrast to the conceptualizing processes associated with Introverted Intuiting. But this cat is quite tired, having exhausted itself trying to do everything for the others.

As it is described and understood here by Christine, this dream highlights the emergence of her inferior function brought about by the tertiary function: the mother cat giving birth to the five kittens. Her unconscious reassures her about the work that she has undertaken and indicates that she is moving in the right direction. For Christine, it is strong encouragement to continue on the path she has chosen. It will gradually bring her to detach more and more from her Extraverted Feeling, which tends to be invasive, and this will give her some distance. As the Aware Ego becomes stronger, a new balance will be seen in more practical ways in Christine's life.

Ferrari or Horse and Buggy?

In the preceding section (Active Imagination), we met Robert, Ni/Te (INTJ), who introduced us to his Auto-Pilot. He is now at a turning point in his career. After having worked very intensely, should he now slow down, because he is not far from retirement age? Should he start out again in a new sphere of activity? Over a period of days, he has the following dream sequence:

First dream:

> I dream that I'm driving a Ferrari, but the road is narrow, very twisty, unpaved. So I can't drive the car at top speed. I come across an old gentleman farmer who offers his horse and buggy to me.

If Robert is unclear about the choices before him, his unconscious offers him a striking alternative! But which choice should he make? Then he has another dream.

Second dream:

> I'm driving quietly along a road. I'm stopped by a policeman. I'm astounded.
> "Why did you pull me over?"
> "You were speeding."
> *"Me?"*
> "Yes, over 80 miles an hour."
> *"No way!"*
> "Yes. Are you aware of the speed limit?"
> *"60?"*
> "No."
> *"50?"*
> "No. 30 miles an hour. You are within the village limits."
> I can't get over this. I thought I was driving along doing the speed limit; I must have been hypnotized by the road. The cop asks me if it's the first time that I've ever gotten a speeding ticket. I tell him yes. So he just gives me a recorded warning, and he tells me that next time there will be a large fine.

Robert's Auto-Pilot has a tendency to get caught up in things. He moves along so quickly because he is obsessed with the work to be done, and he doesn't take the time for simple relationships (the villagers). His unconscious sends him a warning; it is in his own best interests to heed the warning, otherwise the consequences will be much more detrimental. The Auto-Pilot would love to be in the Ferrari, but that can be very dangerous. A different pace is required. So what about the horse and buggy? Robert's unconscious is even more clever in the next dream:

Third dream:

> I'm about to park my car at Capitol Hill. I see xxx, a former President for whom I worked previously, walking along the

sidewalk. I stop and get out of the car to greet him. He asks what I've been up to. I say that I'm advisor to the new President. He then asks: "When are you finally going to be President yourself instead of always advisor?"

The dream encourages Robert not to "drive" for anyone but himself. He must find his own path. But to do this, he has to call on new resources. And that's his fourth dream:

Fourth dream:

> I took part in a bidding process limited to three companies; we put in a bid on a large urbanization project. I won. I am in the middle of a crowd of the candidates and spectators, etc., and I'm very pleased. I am next to one of the losers. Although he doesn't look like me at all, he is my twin. He blocks my path; he's angry; he says I took advantage of information that he didn't have. I say that I just went to the Public Works Department. He says it's scandalous, because he didn't do that. I say that it is a public service, and that someone who doesn't know that they are there to answer questions shouldn't even be submitting bids.

Robert's dominant function, Introverted Intuiting, wanted to solve the problem on its own – and it lost. The "Robert" who won is much more devious: he went to get the information at its source. This practical ability to seek out useful external information, without being weighed down with assumptions or being limited to its own resources – this comes from Extraverted Sensing, Robert's inferior function.

This series of dreams obviously doesn't tell Robert what to do. But it gives him some very clear indications about avoiding excess and about new resources that he can make use of. In other words, his unconscious contributes in its own way to the emergence of Robert's Aware Ego.

Now It's Your Turn!

Volumes have been written on dream interpretation. The significance of dreams has, without a doubt, interested humans since the dawn of time: what wouldn't we give to finally have the key to interpreting dreams? Here, we limit ourselves to the principal elements.

Write Down Your Dreams

- Write down your dreams in a special notebook or computer file; by doing this, their importance is clear, and they will not be lost.
- Keep this notebook and a pen (some are equipped with a built-in light!) next to your bed to be able to jot down, even late at night, the two or three key words that will help you remember the dream upon waking.
- Review it; relive the dream several times in your head before writing it down.
- Write it down as soon as possible after you have woken; tell your bedpartner about it if he or she is interested.
- Draw it, recreate it, sculpt it, remake it in whichever medium inspires you.

Understand Your Dreams

- Take your time: the meaning of a dream sometimes only appears after a period of maturation, like decanting a wine.
- Keep contact with the dream elements and the feelings that arose, without attempting to understand the dream intellectually.
- A dream is polysemic – it can have many meanings; it may open the door to several different interpretations that are not mutually exclusive. The dream summarized above, in which Robert is stopped for speeding, could also be a reminder to him that he drives too quickly and that he is running the risk of having an accident or losing his license!

- A series of dreams is often more enlightening than an isolated dream. The unconscious is telling a story and the dreams are the chapters.
- Recurring dreams are particularly important: they emphasize a point that the dreamer does not understand. A change in a recurring dream is always pertinent; in general, it means that an answer to a question raised by the dream has been integrated.
- The dream may have significance related to an external reality:

> Karina is sued by a neighbor with malicious intentions. Certain of her legal rights and the righteousness of her situation, Karina does not see the need to call a lawyer, believing she can present her case herself. A few days before the hearing, she dreams that she is going to lose the trial. Deeply troubled, she decides to make an emergency call to a lawyer. It is definitely a move in the right direction because the plaintiff raises procedural arguments that Karina could not have dealt with, and which would most certainly have caused her to lose the trial. Supported by her lawyer, not only does she win her case, but the plaintiff must pay costs.

- However, in general, we can hypothesize that all elements of the dream are representative of the dreamer. The characters who appear are not there for themselves, but rather to represent a part of the dreamer. This is a particularly sensitive topic in two types of dream which can frequently trouble some individuals:
    - The dreamer dreams that he is making love to someone other than his partner. It is pointless to feel guilty for this dream-state adultery! The dream indicates much more probably that the dreamer is making an alliance or a connection with a new part of himself. So it becomes interesting to try to understand what this new "person" represents for the dreamer.
    - The dreamer dreams that he is tortured or killed by someone (or the opposite, that he tortures or kills someone else). There is no point crying foul! The unconscious is indicating that one part of the dreamer is oppressing another part. Then we must simply discover which two parts are involved.

> *In summary*
>
> The approach of Intelligence of Self is founded on proven methods. It is not just wishful thinking here, but practices which are even more effective if they are used regularly.
>
> It may prove useful at the beginning, and at certain other stages, to benefit from the help of a professional; however, each of us walks the path alone.
>
> For this reason, the last chapter deals with self-coaching, or how an individual working alone can use the approach and the accompanying methods.

8

SELF-COACHING THROUGH THE INSIGHTS OF INTELLIGENCE OF SELF

BEYOND THE METHOD AND THE TECHNIQUES, Intelligence of Self is a way of life, a means of understanding our existence and making progress along our path, our road to individuation. It requires a constant and benevolent awareness about what is going on in our life so that we can understand "who is speaking" within us, who is at the controls.

For this reason, the goal of the current chapter is to present what each one of us can accomplish working alone pursuing our own personal growth. Of course, help – from a coach, consultant, or therapist – would be very useful. It is often even necessary, in times of difficulty, or in order to learn the different techniques that we have described. Input from a professional helps us avoid wasting precious time and deluding ourselves about our Self and our self-development, which is so easy to do if we are working alone. However, other than some specific cases, there is no reason to think that we will be getting into a lifelong coaching or therapy experience.

Throughout the book, we have presented the various aspects of Intelligence of Self, either through its underlying principles or through the tools which enable us to apply the principles. We will review and summarize them here, from the angle of how they can be used by someone working on their own. We refer the reader to previous sections of this book for the complete details. We will follow the order of the three laws of development presented in Chapter 3:

- Identifying or Naming,
- Disidentifying or "Unhooking"
- Integrating and Rebalancing the Opposites.

But prior to continuing, here are a few practical tips.

PRACTICAL TIPS

Which Part of Us Wishes to Undertake This Work?

This is the first question to ask, and it contains the seed from which the rest of the work will evolve. Is it the Aware Ego continuing along its path? Or a Sub-Personality? And if so, which one? Could it be:

- The Perfectionist, who thinks it must always do better,
- The Self-development Enthusiast, who has made a religion of it,
- The Follower, because it's the newest trend,
- Or is it one of the many others…?

If one Sub-Personality is alone at the controls, it's very unlikely that the Aware Ego will develop. This is equivalent to the distinction made by the Palo Alto school between Level 1 changes, where it is only the content that changes, and Level 2 changes, where it is the process itself that changes[24]. And similarly, there is the example cited by Marie-Louise von Franz[25] about the professor of natural sciences, an Introverted Thinking type: wishing to develop his Feeling side, he dreams of specific, rare, alpine flowers, representative of his inferior function, Feeling. But he then undertakes a project to collect and classify these flowers, simply continuing in accordance with the operating mode of his dominant function.

Take Your Time

Embracing the opposite poles and developing an Aware Ego are not simple mechanistic processes, related through cause and effect and where we can expect an immediate result once the cause has been triggered. It is much more like gardening. Clearly we must prepare the terrain, fertilize, water, and ensure adequate sunlight, but the plant grows according to its own rhythm, and pulling on the plant to make it grow faster serves no purpose.

---

[24] See for example *Pragmatics of Human Communication*, Paul Watzlawick et al., 1967

[25] ML von Franz *The Inferior Function in Jung's Typology* 1971 Spring 1986

Use or Create Favorable Moments

We cannot spend our time analyzing ourselves; life is first meant to be lived. We are in the river; we can't spend all our time on the shore watching ourselves swim.

On the other hand, it isn't easy to understand what is happening if we are constantly in the rapids. We must seize the opportunities that arise in order to step back and take a breather. Often the periods of upheaval and change (in a relationship or at work) can be beneficial opportunities. We must know how to make these moments happen as well: on a journey, the stopover is also part of the trip.

Work with Others

Personal development is not necessarily a solitary undertaking; quite to the contrary, interpersonal exchanges and bonds forged within a group can often magnify things, giving meaning and depth to the work of each person.

Three groups may play this role, each somewhat differently.

Friends

Sharing experiences and speaking in confidence about ourselves and our emotions enables us to step back and objectivize our feelings. Having someone listen to us attentively is already an invaluable support.

Intimate Relationships (Couples)

If both partners love each other deeply and share a common will to continue evolving, they are each obliged, in walking the same path, to learn to accept each other's differences, to take back the projections that they put onto each other, and to become more and more themselves, so that they can each love the other for who they truly are and not just for what they bring to the relationship.

A Therapy Group

This offers a "sounding board" unlike any other; it enables us to deepen our understanding of others, and it offers support, challenge, and encouragement, all at once.

As well, in a greater sense, any encounter – a stranger on the bus or a school friend rediscovered after many years – offers us the chance to take a look back on our life, reflect on its meaning, and expand our knowledge of Self and understanding of others.

IDENTIFY YOUR OPERATING SYSTEM

Identify Your Personality Type

If it is particularly useful to use a questionnaire[26] and to have the help of a practitioner qualified in this area, it is nonetheless possible to get an initial idea of one's type through the descriptions given in our books.

Here are some possibilities.

Start from the 8 Functions

The eight psychic functions are described in the first chapter of this book. They can be divided into two groups:

- The Perceiving functions:
    - Extraverted Sensing
    - Introverted Sensing
    - Extraverted Intuiting
    - Introverted Intuiting
- The Judging functions:
    - Extraverted Thinking
    - Introverted Thinking
    - Extraverted Feeling
    - Introverted Feeling

---

[26] Such as the CCTI, Cailloux-Cauvin Type Indicator

In each of these groups there is typically a function that we use more easily or more naturally than the others. Start by identifying these two preferred functions.

Then look at each one and identify which is the most familiar to you of the two you have chosen – the one that describes you the best. This is the dominant function, and the other is the auxiliary. By following these steps, you can "create" your type, as we did earlier – for example Ni/Fe for Introverted Intuiting (dominant), Extraverted Feeling (auxiliary).

Start from the 4 Dimensions and the 8 Polarities

This is the most traditional approach to personality type[27]. By following this route, you will write your type with the initial letters of the preferred polarities, using one for each of the four dimensions. For example ENFJ, which is the equivalent code for Ni/Fe.

Use the Function Cross

Whichever approach you take, you can refer back to Chapter 1, Table 1.10, which summarizes all the types, and then complete your own function cross. Being able to clearly identify the first two functions is quite sufficient at this stage! You will be able to return to the others at your leisure.

Read through the tables in Chapter 1 to see if the descriptions of the dominant and auxiliary functions can be applied to you and your two preferred functions[28].

---

[27] You will find detailed descriptions in our books *Deviens qui tu es* and *Les types de personnalité*.

[28] If you wish to pursue your analysis further, *Deviens qui tu es* contains practical exercises

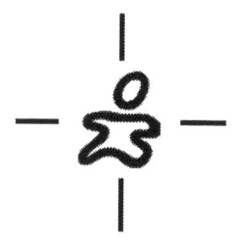

Figure 8.1 – Your Function Cross
Identify Your Primary Strategies

Groups of Strategies

The fundamental or primary strategies are based on each of us as individuals, our environment, and our adaptation to it. However, we have observed that there are some large groups or "families" of related strategies.

These were described in Chapter 2. Review them to discover which ones are closest to your way of doing things. Observe how the strategies have developed within you – there will be similarities and differences.

Self-observation

Notice the following:

- Your "automatic" behaviors: what you do without thinking about it because "that's how I do it", "it's obvious", or "that's the only way to do it".
- The things you do well and quickly, where you have fast, efficient methods for achieving results.
- Any changes in energy level or mood, which indicate that a different part of you is taking control.
- The circumstances that cause these changes.

Recognizing the Auto-Pilot

The Auto-Pilot is a combination of preferred functions and strategies; it unites a good number of the characteristics you've identified. Its major feature is undoubtedly mistaking itself for you.

When we say "I" – as in "I'm like that, I'm honest, I don't like people who..." – we can be almost certain that it's our Auto-Pilot that is speaking. Listen carefully for these "I" statements. They describe how you probably are most of the time, even if you are unaware of it.

Other indicators hint at the Auto-Pilot's presence:

- Recall any nicknames you were given as a child. Although these nicknames are far too often expressed in a critical or negative manner, both nicknames and "totems" emphasize our prominent features; they are partial, often biased, but they can be a useful indicator to consider.
- Imagine the congratulatory speech that your employer might make upon your departure or at your retirement dinner. Employers generally like to do business with our Auto-Pilot, which interests them because it is efficient and relatively uncomplicated.

Finding Your Disowned Selves

These disowned parts are the opposite of the Auto-Pilot, so if you have identified your Auto-Pilot, you know that you need to look in the opposite direction to find these poorly integrated or unintegrated parts.

Along the way, we have described the two main approaches relating to the disowned Selves.

- With respect to the inferior function, we have shown the principal ways it manifests: inconsistency, slowness, awkwardness, repeated errors, oversensitivity, irritability. This can be accompanied by feelings of shame or guilt, as the Auto-Pilot is totally unable to appreciate these contributions. Look carefully at the areas in which these manifestations occur. They are a sign of our areas of difficulty, or parts that we are not aware of or that we reject.

- And to continue further, becoming aware of our projections is the royal road that brings us to the point where we can clearly see both the judging parts of us and the parts that are judged and that we project onto others. We strongly encourage you to do this work – the results are as useful as they are surprising. The practical steps for this are described in the previous chapter.

DISIDENTIFYING THE AUTO-PILOT

"Naming" and "disidentifying" are closely linked:

- In order to create distance or detach from a dominant part, we must begin by identifying it, naming it;
- But by actually naming it, we give it an identity other than "I/me" and this triggers the process of disidentification.

The process of disidentification is therefore paradoxically going to require that we identify more and more clearly the parts of us that tend to mistake themselves for us. Identifying and detaching are two parts of the same process, which can be nurtured in several ways. We will describe or review these in the next section. No one way is better than the others; it falls to each individual to choose the way(s) which suit him best at any given moment, with complete flexibility to change at his discretion.

Representation of the Dominant Part

In order to succeed in identifying the dominant part within and to detach from it, it is very useful to make a physical representation of it, thus giving it a form of existence other than verbal, for example:

- Draw it. It's not about creating a work of art, but rather giving it form. Judicious use of the "other hand" (the right for lefties; the left for righties) can be made in order to feel freer, avoid any esthetic judgments, and let the unconscious express itself better.

- Sculpt it. Use the material that suits you best – stone, wood, modeling dough, clay, paper mâché....
- Dance it. Let your body express the energy of this part; do this in front of a mirror in order to get the necessary distance, or film it and view the dance afterward.
- Find a meaningful object which symbolizes it.

The same can be done with the parts you are unaware of, in order to integrate them more completely.

These representations must continue to exist beyond the limits of this exercise. Depending on their size, we can slip them into our Day-Timer, put them on a corner of our desk or night table or any other location that seems appropriate. The goal is to keep them in our awareness so we can recognize when they are surreptitiously sliding into the control seat.

Active Imagination

We described this method in detail in Chapter 7. Here, we will simply emphasize the effectiveness of this approach – which requires us to establish a well-defined time and space where we do not run the risk of being disturbed.

Dreams

The same holds true for dream work, which we also discussed in Chapter 7. We stress that the goal is not to "interpret" our dreams in a systematic and willful manner but rather to pay attention to them and to the messages they bring forth from our unconscious, letting them unfurl within us.

Daily Life

These methods we have just mentioned are interesting in and of themselves: they enable us to recognize and detach from our primary parts in order to then be able to spot them more easily when they show up in everyday life.

The Auto-Pilot has, in fact, a great talent for showing up unannounced, without asking permission or even giving a warning, and quite often we are completely unaware of its presence. We are not suggesting stopping it from getting involved – the Auto-Pilot is far too useful for us to do without it. It is simply a matter of knowing, when it is around, whether we should let it act on our behalf, or whether we should proceed differently. As a result, the sooner we can spot it poking up its nose, the more able we will be to decide who should be acting.

In Chapter 3, we described the visible characteristics of the eight functions and the way they appear in practical terms. As our Auto-Pilot principally makes use of just one of the functions, it definitely takes on some of those features. It is worth a moment of our time to go into this in more detail here. Here are some aspects we should pay particular attention to:

- voice: tone, register, speed, rhythm
- posture: upright, stiff, relaxed, supple, hunched over, grounded or unbalanced, fixed in one place, agitated
- arm movements: their energy, the range of motion
- head carriage: bent forward, arched backward, fluid, frozen
- eye contact: direct, fleeting, seeking the horizon, upward, to the rear, to the side.

It is striking to see that each Sub-Personality has its own energy, to such a degree that observers and even clients are completely amazed at the uniqueness of each Part. So the more you are aware of the distinct ways in which the various Sub-Personalities manifest, the more you will be able to be your own true pilot and make choices and decisions from a more balanced perspective.

INTEGRATING THE SHADOW

Once you have been able to disidentify from your Auto-Pilot, the opposite poles can be integrated. Remember that we are not talking about some type of psychic muscle-building. It is more like the phenomenon of communicating vessels: the opposite pole spontaneously fills the space left vacant by the dominant pole. Or more precisely, the person feels a sense of expansion, becoming greater than the Sub-Personality believed him to be.

What's more, it is possible to help this process along. Here are two ways to achieve this.

The Teaspoon

Integrating the opposite pole is often seen by the dominant Sub-Personality as an impossible or very difficult task. We feel like we must become someone else, or that we must be able to do everything that the opposite pole makes possible. This is probably a Perfectionist showing up, and it makes us believe that if we haven't achieved everything, we haven't achieved anything.

This is false. The goal is not to transform everything, nor is it to do *anything* all at once. It is possible to eat an elephant – just not all at one sitting. We need to move ahead gradually. For this reason, the best question to ask oneself is the following: "What could I do that I don't do now, or what could I do better than I do now if I were to take a small teaspoon of the opposite pole?" You can also think of this as a homeopathic dose, or a few drops of an essential oil, or whatever metaphor makes sense to you.

What matters most is to become very clear about what really needs improving, and to do this in very small doses. After a period of time, you will be amazed at the distance you have traveled – because the doses have a cumulative effect and permit a progressive rebalancing.

The Regulator of Opposites

This deliberate undertaking is intended to let you embrace the opposite poles and balance them. It can be practised as an exercise by following the directions given here. This can be done at any time, most naturally after there has been some contact with two opposite Sub-Personalities, such as during an active imagination session.

- Sit comfortably. Become aware of your breath, without trying to modify it. Find a state of relaxation, however you prefer to do this.
- Mentally picture your Auto-Pilot, or the Sub-Personality that is inhabiting you right now.

- In your mind, place this Sub-Personality somewhere in the room, in the location that seems most natural for it.
- Look closely at its appearance; describe it with all the features and details that you have noticed or given it in other exercises.
- Somewhere between you and the Sub-Personality, imagine a "regulator" or control which enables you to increase or decrease the intensity of this Sub-Personality. The control can be any form you prefer: a tap, a valve, a thermostat or any other image that you desire.
- Use this regulator to increase the Sub-Personality's energy level. Stop when you feel that it might overwhelm you.
- And again, with the regulator, decrease the energy, without losing contact with the Sub-Personality.
- Repeat this increase/decrease several times.
- Decrease the primary Sub-Personality's energy to its lowest level.
- Welcome in the opposite pole, the unknown Sub-Personality.
- Invite it to find the most natural location in the room, preferably symmetrical in relation to the dominant pole.
- Look closely at its appearance; describe it with all the features and details that you have noticed or given it in other exercises.
- Somewhere between you and the Sub-Personality, imagine a "regulator" or control which enables you to increase or decrease the intensity of this Sub-Personality. The control can be any form you prefer: a tap, a valve, a thermostat or any other image that you desire. It can be the same as for the dominant Sub-Personality, or it can be different.
- Use this regulator to increase the unknown Sub-Personality's energy level without going beyond a level that is comfortable for you.
- And again, with the regulator, decrease the energy, without losing contact with the Sub-Personality.
- Maintain the unknown Sub-Personality's energy at a level which is comfortable for you.
- While maintaining this energy level, use the regulator to increase the dominant Sub-Personality's energy.

- Bring the dominant Sub-Personality's energy to a level which is comfortable for you.
- Embrace the two poles. Play slightly with the energy levels.
- Let any arising images wash over you.
- Thank the two Sub-Personalities for having participated in the exercise.
- Gradually lower the energy for both Sub-Personalities to zero.
- Stay in the energy of the Aware Ego; take note of what you are feeling.

9

INTELLIGENCE OF SELF IN ACTION

INTRODUCTION

OVER THE YEARS, since its inception near the end of the 1990s, Intelligence of Self has developed further; there are more and more varied and numerous applications of it owing to the dozens of practitioners who use the approach.

We have asked several of these practitioners to outline some of the initiatives they have taken; this is not intended as an exhaustive overview, but simply as a few examples among many. This chapter presents:

- a description of what can be achieved within just one session (Isabelle Demeure);
- an illustration of how coaching can be conducted over several sessions (Isabelle Saint-Macary);
- an example of what Intelligence of Self can bring to mediation (Hélène Dercourt);
- the way in which Intelligence of Self can be used with couples or professional associates (Héloïse Blain)
- an example of a Bonding Pattern between business associates (Delphine Tariot);
- an application with groups of students (Raphaël Bary); and
- a concrete example of work on projections, at both the individual and group levels (Carole Dehais).

REFRAMING A DIFFICULTY IN ONE SESSION

Isabelle Demeure

In order to be able to reframe a problem within one strategic session, be it a review, a coaching session, or a therapy session, there must be "resonance and echo" – in other words, there is one very specific point that the selected process can impact (it "resonates"), and there is also a connection to a larger context (the harmonic "echo") for the client. Sometimes it is a word or a tone of voice or an emotion that is experienced, and these signify that the situation is being viewed from a new perspective, and that a new range of options is opening up.

Intelligence of Self is such a powerful tool that it can create this turnabout within one session alone, enabling one to rethink a situation in a completely different manner and very quickly find a new solution.

Amelia is 40 years old; she studied computer science at university; she recently financed her own MBA and was awarded best dissertation for her thesis. She works in a large American bank and is head of a team of 12 others responsible for quality and methods initiatives.

Amelia has a progressive handicap which is starting to impede her professional advancement. Her hearing is deteriorating, and this is a factor which isolates her and prevents her from feeling fully at ease in some areas of her job. She is brilliant, recognized for her hard work and ambition, and her employer is aware of the situation and wants to continue investing in her career. She was therefore offered a career review and coaching sessions.

She discovers, much to her interest, that her psychological type is Ti/Ne (INTP).

In fact, she is curious about theories in general; she looks for the logic underlying all situations; she is very analytical and critical; she is an expert in her IT field and recognized as such. But, as she also confirms, and which corresponds to her tertiary and inferior functions, she lacks a practical sense, she is not always realistic, and she has difficulty taking her own emotions and those of others into consideration. As a result, she tends to distance herself from her feelings and doesn't communicate them; at work where the problems related to her hearing are mounting, she feels caught in a trap and doesn't know how to free herself.

I have therefore been working with her to create a very objective vision of her career and skills in order to help her regain confidence in herself from a logical standpoint. She is able to make a connection between what she loved to do as a child and still loves working on. She looks back over her evaluations and can clearly see the generalized satisfaction from all members of her working group. She is gradually able to identify the things she can no longer do: teleconferences and large group discussions, particularly in Spanish, her second language. She slowly sketches out her professional target zone around the things she loves doing and does very well: strategizing, improving current processes, conceptualizing products to meet specific needs....

As she becomes more trusting of the coach, she reveals how discouraged she feels about her efforts to move ahead in a future which she feels holds no promise for her. I suggest to her that she change seats in order to meet and listen to this part of her.

Sinking deeply into the sofa, she is sad, unmoving, murmuring softly to herself; she sits there, pitiful to see. Her gaze is unfocused, her words barely audible, her eyes shine with tears.

Amelia (Victim) – *"It's not fair; 'Luckily she's married and has already had her kids', as her mother would say! How is it possible to go on with such a loss? Where will this lead?"*

She complains and feels victimized by a terrible fate; she can't see any way left for her to advance in her career. Her attitude changes and her appearance is all about evasion, indifference: she is exhausted, ready to be done with it all, avoiding all encounters and direct glances as if to show everyone that she doesn't give a darn about all the things that are said that she can't hear.

Amelia (Defeatist) – *"I'm not fighting anymore; I'm leaving, and I don't care who knows!"*

In fact, this new part, which she names the Defeatist, suggests flight as a strategy in order to avoid facing the problem, and for this reason, it moves away physically.

Coach – *"Yes, but Amelia, what is exhausting you so much?"*

A new energy replies, trying at first to sit in the central seat. I invite it to take a different spot so as to distinguish it clearly from the other voices and from Amelia. It stands behind the central armchair; it is a female Zorro standing tall and explaining the vast amount of work it has to accomplish.

Amelia (Zorro) – "Move along! There is nothing to see, just her! What a job trying to make everyone think that Amelia is just like the others: smiling, pretending to understand, being good-humored, friendly, lively, involved, always on top of things, available. And she's so aware of her own strength, of everything she's done to succeed professionally and to fit in socially. But there's always pressure to get the "best" results, and she is always worried about keeping her makeup on and her "mask" in place to hide everything, and now she knows that one day, she will lose the game, and the mask will fall."

Returning to the central seat from which she can review everything that has happened, and survey the Victim, the Defeatist and the exhausting Zorro, she is amazed at these lively and very welcome facets of herself that she has met – she can recognize them and thank them. But she adds:

Amelia – "Yes, I knew all that, but I don't know how to cope with it all, and things really aren't going well at all.

At this point another new Sub-Personality appears – the Lawyer, standing, in black robes, speaking out clearly, authoritatively, with a file filled with facts and tangible proof tucked under its arm.

Amelia (Lawyer) – "You see, ladies and gentlemen, we are no longer in Utopia – there are things to consider. Amelia must have help: there will be no more audio conferences, no more bilingual meetings, because that is the most difficult for her. It will be necessary to support her in certain areas so that she can move into the position she desires. There are many areas where she can excel, and all this, I require, I want for her, I proclaim it loudly and clearly. She has a limitation which requires her to fight, and it's my role to protect her...."

This session was decisive.

Of course, we can keep working to ground ourselves, to dig deeper, go further, but given the demands of a business enterprise, which requires concrete, tangible, observable, rapid results, we can't help but be impressed by this marvelous tool that is Intelligence of Self: consider that in just one session, Amelia was able to find her tipping point, which helped her permanently discard her isolating façade – a courageous but exhausting strategy – to discover a new and deliberate ownership of the situation which will be much more effective in the long run.

At work, everything has changed for her – better relationships with her boss, her isolation has decreased considerably and... guess what she has just done?

She's signed up for acting lessons!

COACHING WITH INTELLIGENCE OF SELF

Isabelle Saint-Macary

Vincent, a senior executive in a large company calls on me to assist him undertake a significant functional and organizational change of his branch of management. It is composed of nine operational co-workers and five managerial co-workers who all report to him.

Vincent meets me and describes the problems: a tense economic situation, increasingly aggressive competition, and the company's current global position and internal organization which, as they currently stand, can no longer meet the challenges.

Vincent – "We are in a difficult situation – the managing director is putting a lot of pressure on me. I've been trying hard for the last year to let everyone know about the need to question everything, and to change attitudes. I'm hoping to get my staff involved in the changes and in reorganizing, but it's a waste of time – they refuse to budge.... I'm exhausted and I don't know what to do!"

The goal of the coaching sessions is therefore to help him get those reporting to him to evolve in the areas of organization, jobs (some or all), and evaluation of methods and tools, etc., with the ultimate goal of bringing about a global change of attitude.

Coach – "I'm going to ask you to describe to me your vision of the situation and explain to me how you went about your efforts, and what is blocking your point of view. To do this, we are first going to work from a personality type indicator, the CCTI, in order to enable you to understand your spontaneous, natural mode of operation in relation to this situation and in the larger context of your life.

Vincent – "*OK, I trust you – let's do it.*"

His profile Fe/Si (ESFJ) appears crystal clear to him. I ask him questions at length to verify that we are dealing with his natural psychological preferences and not with behaviors which were acquired so long ago that they could, in fact, be taken for preferences....

You will find a description of the ESFJ profile in Chapter 1: Tables 1.9 (Extraverted Feeling) and 1.4 (Introverted Sensing). Two characteristics of this type apply in particular to Vincent:

- acting in a determined manner to create an environment that considers the needs of those around him;
- memorizing precise and detailed data.

There are two other growth areas that Vincent should develop:

- having a clear idea of the potential of others;
- using impartial logic to understand them.

We run through his current employment situation in the light of his profile, and a glimmer of comprehension dawns in his eyes, then softens. He realizes that his vision of things is truly his own vision, but there are others....

Vincent – "*But that's exactly me! I'm careful to do a good job, to explain, to be present for my guys.... I surely got that from my training! I'm serious, hardworking, and I know the job really well. I see things in very concrete terms, and I know how to talk and negotiate with clients.*"

Coach – "*I suggest that we review the development path of your type and connect that with your current professional situation.*"

We go over the development path of his type, which is the opposite profile Ti/Ne – INTP (Chapter 1, Tables 1.8 and 1.5). He reads the profile and discovers radical differences. In fact, the characteristics of type Ti/Ne are:

- logically organizing global systems to understand the world;
- examining ideas and information with a sense of curiosity; extrapolating ideas for the future.

Vincent – "Of course! That type is very different from me! Big Talkers and Know-it-Alls! 'Ya gotta do this...ya hafta do that...!' Long speeches about the future, a prestigious position, and who cares about the reality of business! OK, so I can see now that I have to be clearer, and I have to give a more precise sense of direction to my Agency executives, and I should definitely be stricter, less understanding...."

We "play" with Vincent's opposite, by having his Ti/Ne (INTP) side express its vision for his professional situation: there are so many different ways to see the same situation! To do this, I suggest to Vincent that he move out of his usual seat in my office and choose a different location to step into this new energy in order to facilitate grounding this facet of his personality. Vincent gets up and comes to sit on another chair, located quite noticeably behind his usual armchair. From that location he speaks up:

Vincent – "I work alone in my office; I decide on the project, and this one is ambitious! I'm diplomatic and strategic; I let my colleagues work autonomously by setting the goals and counting on their competency and sense of responsibility...."

The coach invites Vincent to return to the central chair.

Coach – "Well, Vincent, now that you have a broader perspective, how does what you just said through the INTP profile strike you, when you consider your organizational change project?"

Vincent – "I realize that I most certainly haven't formalized the vision behind this reorganization by putting it into writing or communicating it clearly enough.... I am too focused on achieving consensus among my co-workers because they are hardworking and loyal! But I know I should be stricter and explain that they don't have a choice. I do a lot of work for them, and I let them work at their own speed because I trust them! When they have problems or they don't do the work, I make excuses for them, and I go back again and explain what they have to do...."

We begin the development process with Vincent to gradually integrate this opposite profile; this will allow him to be more thorough when he undertakes the planning and implementation of the upcoming changes.

In the following sessions, we concentrate on each important area of his professional situation one after the other: his oral and written communications addressed to his staff, his local and off-site executives, the organization of the sectors that he oversees, his collaborators, the competition, the key internal and external contacts, economic impact, etc....

At each session, we deal with or review different points. Vincent speaks spontaneously – as an ESFJ, this is first nature to him, his dominant function. This energy takes a seat very close to the central armchair (about 12 inches to the left of it). When he calls on his "countertype", INTP, which is still very difficult to access, I invite it to physically move to another location. So it sits in a completely different spot, well behind the central seat. He gradually integrates, experiences, lives through this facet of himself. And then from the central position, he is able to feel and visualize the differences, observe what challenges him, and what he intends to do at each point as he continues to make progress.

When we meet next, he explains what he has accomplished. I ask him about what happened (what was easy, or difficult, feedback on his experiences), and what he observed in the others he interacts with. He makes progress, discovering what his new behaviors and ways of acting and communicating are bringing him. As the days pass, he feels more confident and expresses satisfaction with these new experiences.

Vincent – "I've set up a series of informative meetings for all of the Agencies in order to communicate the objectives of the reorganization and to explain clearly what is at stake and what new directions we'll be taking. The feedback was quite positive, and I realized that my Agency directors (my staff) don't know how to communicate! I'm going to meet with them all individually so that they can make a presentation of their plans to reorganize within their own Agency.... And then I created a management committee to take care of progress reports and to work together on ways to cooperate with managerial services. But it's tough, because my Agency directors aren't moving ahead very quickly, and they grumble about attending meetings.... I still tend to let them off too easily and solve things for them!"

Coach – "It's quite normal, Vincent, your opposite parts or different parts are struggling against each other. You need to give each of them space. As you've observed, it's the two of them taken together which will enable you to complete this organizational change successfully. This will also help you to develop your talents as a leader and to integrate new management styles. And maybe your staff will also change in a kind of domino effect! Have you noticed how your initiatives might be impacting them?

Vincent – "The Agencies' employees were thrilled to be given the information and to be able to exchange ideas with me. The Agency executives were relieved that I'm handling the speeches and focusing on what will upset employees and the organization within each Agency, or potentially even impact all jobs. By going out in the field, I've been able to see and understand a lot more!"

Coach – "Well done, Vincent. In your opinion, which parts of you were involved in these actions?"

Vincent – "Easy – for communication and interaction, my ESFJ! And that also goes for the fact that I was able to see a ton of things that need to be changed. But I know what you're getting at! I'm not going to do things that should be done by the my directors. I will call on my INTP, write a comprehensive email to outline my analysis, and ask them to act!"

The note of satisfaction in his voice is significant. In fact, in the early stages of learning, it takes a considerable effort and significant energy to generate new behaviors and actions and to persevere with them. As the new resources are integrated, we start to see the client expressing a degree of pleasure and satisfaction in using them.

However, from the Coach's perspective, there remains the task of helping him access these new Parts of himself on a regular basis.

Coach – "Vincent, how can you continue to benefit from all of these Sub-Personalities that we have met together?"

Vincent – "I've learned one thing: twice a day for about an hour I make myself close the door of my office – it's usually always open! This forces me to settle down, work on my files, bring myself back into the present, and calm down; then I write notes, comments, emails to clarify my expectations and to inform others. The rest of the time, I'm in my comfort zone – I'm in touch with everyone: staff, clients, etc...."

In the language of Intelligence of Self, I help him achieve an elasticity of Self so that he does not have to act exclusively from his innate, preferred Self (ESFJ), even if this is very useful and effective. This type, like any other type, is not initially sufficient – at times our dominant type can even block us or prevent us from seeing events or situations in a larger context. We then work on developing his "360-degree vision" to enable him to view situations from a variety of different angles.

Intelligence of Self is an organic process which helps the client become aware of the limitations of his Auto-Pilot, which may have been controlling his life or work in the past. This permits the client to let his potential shine through and utilize a more balanced skill set to face the task at hand.

In order for these changes to endure, during every session we work on different grounding techniques: visualization, feeling emotions, creating images, naming, etc. These become new resources linked to the innate profile (Fe/Si, ESFJ) and the opposite (Ti/Ne, INTP) to give Vincent the option of calling on each as needed, depending on the situation. And so he was able to build his organizational vision for change from a much wider perspective, and he was able to integrate new elements.

We met again several months after the end of his coaching sessions, and he spoke of his new way of doing things:

Vincent – "When I have doubts or I'm hesitating, I take some alone time to call on all my resources to listen to them and observe them and deal with the question that is bothering me. It's only afterwards that I can see and clearly choose what I need to do and define how I need to act.... Sometimes I find that my natural habits come roaring back, but a few short seconds later, I realize it, and I refocus my efforts!"

INTELLIGENCE OF SELF AND MEDIATION

Hélène Dercourt

Mediation is a conflict resolution tool which aims to bring individuals involved in conflict to a point where they can find a solution together. The two prior conditions for mediation are, on the one hand, a recognition by both parties that there is a conflict, and on the other, a common desire to find a way out of the conflict.

Even though mediation is a form of facilitation, not all facilitations are mediations. For example, some facilitations are designed to help foster self-knowledge by focusing on projections.

Others enable business associates to find answers to specific professional issues (continuing their association, deciding to offer partnership to a new associate...). It is intended to ensure that all associates are included and feel consulted in these high-stakes decisions. We speak of mediation when there is a stated conflict. The facilitation ends when a solution has been found. The mediator must manage the distrust and often pre-existing hostility between the two parties.

In the following example, in an international consulting firm, the manager of a state-level office acquired by the firm 18 months earlier has asked the CEO to let him go.

> Richard (manager), type Fi/Ne – INFP (Introverted Feeling/ Extraverted Intuiting – Tables 1.7 and 1.5 in Chapter 1), and David (CEO), type Te/Si – ESTJ (Extraverted Thinking/ Introverted Sensing – Tables 1.6 and 1.4).

The manager/sailor, Richard, intends to spend a year with his family aboard a boat, while he receives unemployment benefits, and he submits his request to the CEO, David.

> David is surprised, even shocked. He categorically refuses to consider this request. He expresses his reactions to Richard. He thinks it is a rather crooked way for Richard to go about creating a competitor firm, stealing both clients and consultants, while benefiting from the money included in a settlement package. He calls Richard a crook, and says that even if Richard were sincere, which he does not believe, misusing unemployment funds to treat himself to a cruise around the world would be absolutely scandalous.

Richard is humiliated. He wants no further contact with David. He announces his resignation and his decision to delay the boat trip until he can earn the money to afford it. To do this, he will create, as David suggested, a rival company which will target the same clients and draw from the firm's pool of consultants to find its next candidates.

The war is on.

Having researched the question, David realizes that Richard never signed a non-compete clause. In actual fact, Richard was the founding owner's assistant at the time of signing the deal. It was intended all along that the original owner would leave after signing.

For the last 18 months, Richard has been the only link between the international firm and the branch consultants. He is the only one who knows the clients. The financial stakes for the international firm are astronomical: loss of all the money invested in the deal. Powerless, David therefore decides to call in a mediator.

The mediator, as any coach, maintains a neutral, considerate manner. Between the two main characters, trust has been broken, but the personal relationships between the mediator and David and the mediator and Richard will enable the creation of an appropriate level of communication between all parties.

During the encounter with Richard, the mediator discovers that the trip around the world is important for Richard and his family, that it is at an advanced stage of planning, and that his wife has already informed her employer. She expects to leave her job in six months. Richard is in a state of extreme stress, and he accepts the attempt at mediation. The mediator helps him discover his personality type by using the CCTI. The encounter lasts two and a half hours. Some time is required so that a relationship can develop, and so that they can both get in touch with their inner self, something that is not very typical in the world of business.

The encounter with David is an opportunity for the mediator to help him discover his CCTI type as well. David expects that the mediation will, in a structured and logical manner, bring Richard to the point where he can accept and agree with the firm's expectations. In fact, David cannot imagine any other outcome. The individual encounter offers the mediator the chance to remind David that no exit solution exists unless he can find a way to open himself to Richard's way of operating. Right from this first encounter – which shakes David up considerably, as he feels entirely justified in his views – he realizes that this work with the CCTI will bring them both to re-evaluate their viewpoints.

During a standard facilitation, it is more beneficial to have both individuals discover their type at the same session, since the discoveries made by each one shed light on the issues and problems encountered with the personality type of the other. In this particular case, David and Richard's issues are very urgent, and the conflict is so great that they are no longer speaking to one another. Additionally, they scarcely know each other and have had hardly any interaction.

So their type discovery interviews are done individually, and this first phase helps the facilitator build a relationship with each of them.

The first joint mediation session starts on a tense note. With the agreement of both participants, the mediator gives each a description of the other's type (Fi/Ne, INFP for Richard, and Te/Si, ESTJ for David), with elements that help them understand each others' operating differences. In this way, they accomplish something related to the conflict without actually touching on it. Taking the necessary time, the mediator reviews past events in the light of their types, and Richard and David each speak and clarify. Each one opens up about himself and feels heard. The interactions are calmer, and they are both ready to be respectful of the other.

The mediator is responsible for creating a framework for the sessions and will enable each of them to discover himself as well as discover the other. Coming to a fuller awareness of the causes underlying the conflict will make it possible to find a way out.

The second joint mediation session begins with a reformulation exercise.

Richard is the first to speak. He is relieved to be able to express the hurt he felt when David called him dishonest. David reformulates. Having come to the meeting for a specific business objective, David takes the time to connect with his emotions. During the session, it becomes evident that this energy change pleases and amazes him. He is willing to take the time for this.

The current situation is very sensitive. Mediation between individuals related in a hierarchical employer/employee relationship, particularly when the relationship is ongoing, must subtly allow each one to experience the work in an authentic way (and this is an absolute precondition for success), while preserving a somewhat formal, protective relationship for the future. Generally speaking, the depth of the work must be established by the mediator, depending on the circumstances. This method is often used to facilitate work between business associates or former associates. The intensity of the shared journey often allows for very profound work, a deeper understanding of the other, and a true healing of souls.

Becoming Who You Are with the Intelligence of Self

In some cases, one of the parties will ask for a private session after the two-person session. Here as well, it falls to the mediator to evaluate the timeliness of the request. In any case, the option will be discussed by all three, both parties and the mediator, together.

We cannot lose sight of the fact that it is essential for both parties to want to resolve the situation. When they request mediation, the need is often so great that both are ready to do whatever it takes for the process to succeed.

At the end of the second joint session, David is ready to talk about a solution. The mediator stops the session. It is better for them to take a break, having reached this place of mutual understanding. A session is scheduled three days later.

At the third joint session, the topic of finding a solution is broached. Both parties are asked to propose their solutions without commentary. This is to enable the most creative solutions to emerge.

Richard has no suggestions. David speaks up: Richard will remain employed by the firm. For the next six months he will train his replacement. Then he will resign. The firm will pay him for a non-compete clause in the same amount as he would have received in unemployment benefits. At the end of his trip, Richard may, if he wishes, return to the firm. Richard is visibly relieved and accepts at once. David is touched by Richard's immediate agreement.

The deep understanding they have gained of one another creates a mutual trust. They each know that the other will follow through on the project.

Although the mediator never suggests any solutions, he ensures that there is a balance and a durability to the final solution. If one party feels cheated, the mediation has failed, and the future is compromised. Mediation transforms the conflict, a source of stress and disharmony, into an opportunity to deepen one's self-awareness and one's understanding of others, and it quite often makes it possible to restore the reciprocal respect and esteem that have been lost by both parties.

These sessions enable Richard to reaffirm his own values and to convince David that, far from dishonest, he is committed and completely worthy of the trust of others. Richard also recognizes that he does not feel bound by systems and structures – the planned unemployment insurance fraud does not bother him in the least. David listens to Richard's travel plans and is even able to voice his admiration. He admits to being somewhat obsessed with his work and having a hard time imagining anything else but work.

Each is able to acknowledge the other, and they complete the process, both of them having grown as individuals and feeling at ease in their new awareness.

COACHING FOR COUPLES OR ASSOCIATES

Héloïse Blain

Background

Four years earlier, Crystal and Raymond started a business focused on young children – an independent and private Montessori teaching center. The business finances are in the black and have been stable recently. They have been a couple for 15 years, and this is reflected in their mature relationship, which is based on the complementarity of their characters and on a shared vision which helped them create the business.

Crystal had previous experience in business and partnerships. Up to this point, she has dealt with student and parent relations as well as with the curriculum; however, she is beginning to have serious doubts about the soundness of their business. She is aware of the high stakes when it comes to the quality of relationships and the durability of the business: only 52% of all businesses created survive more than five years.[29]

Crystal is the initiator of this coaching request: she notices the negative reactions of some parents who are the main clients of their family business, and she focuses on several recurring complaints along with the deterioration of their work environment and working conditions.

Raymond has always been interested in owning a small business. This is the first time that such an undertaking has been accomplished, and he

---

[29] National Institute of Statistics and Economic Studies (INSEE)

intends to make every effort to ensure that the odds are stacked in their favor to succeed.

Crystal – "I've had it – I can't take this suffocating routine anymore! Sometimes I regret starting up the business together. We work like dogs, and our relationship as a couple has really deteriorated in the last four years."

Raymond – "Hey, no way, you're exaggerating. Things are going well, even if it's not an easy undertaking. There is no reason to worry – we are well equipped to succeed."

Crystal – "It's always the same tension between us, and if this continues, our parents won't sign up their children again and we'll be out of business!"

Raymond – "Why are you so worried? We have the same vision, maybe not exactly the same personal ambitions, that's all. I think there are some Montessori management principles that we could apply directly to our situation. Maria Montessori's methods enable the child to build himself. This is a simple, healthy approach: 'Teach me to do it alone' is certainly something that we can transfer to the field of business management."

Objectives

At the start of the coaching sessions, Crystal and Raymond's expectations are related to three issues:

1. Stabilizing their professional relationship as business partners and reviving their previously close connection;
2. Reassuring parents and clients in order to ensure the long-term viability of the business and the efforts invested;
3. Discovering the secret behind a flourishing couple relationship, and finding the free time to pursue this.

Procedure

In order to meet their different expectations, Crystal and Raymond decide to set up an initial contract of four half-days over the course of three months, followed by a regular coaching session for business partners, on a semi-annual basis. One detail of the approach they have specified is that they will both attend every session as a couple.

Right from the first session Crystal and Raymond are aware that a lot of tension arises when they are required to make decisions and follow through on the ambitious – occasionally impossible – plans that they each devise. This dialogue takes place:

Raymond – "*A decision ripens over time, is based in logic, and is never written in stone!*"

Crystal – "*We already discussed it, we confirmed it a long time ago, and we moved on to the next topic!*"

As they are both present for the personal development work done in turns with the coach, they are able to realize how their personality differences cause major friction when they must make decisions together.

Crystal is an NeFi, ENFP who operates most often like "the Fighter" described on page 36, Figure 2.2. (Extraverted Intuiting/Introverted Feeling – Chapter 1, Tables 1.5 and 1.7). Her professional life has caused her to overvalue her tertiary function, Extraverted Thinking. She therefore has a tendency to act quickly on the basis of new ideas. This is what is expressed when that part speaks up:

Crystal – "*I like to innovate, to make decisions; I like things to move forward. For me 'Where there's a will, there's a way!' I feel like I'm always the one initiating progress. I can't stop taking on new projects because I love this stimulating side, and I can't accept that you aren't on the same wavelength as me.*"

As for Raymond, he is a TiNe, INTP (Introverted Thinking/Extraverted Intuiting – Chapter 1, Tables 1.8 and 1.5). Although new ideas attract him, he needs time to process a decision.

Raymond – "*I like taking my time. I need time to process – for sure don't rush me just for a quick decision! When the time is ripe, a decision can be made clearly and everything goes very quickly, efficiently. Decisions come on their own for me, and they can't always be hurried along by talking about them. And they can always be revisited after the fact.*"

In the course of the sessions, Crystal discovers her Inner Child, closely connected to Introverted Feeling, a part of her that she had no awareness of, or she despised; this helps her connect with her sense of fatigue.

Crystal's Inner Child – "*I'm fed up with her always pushing. I feel overwhelmed. She never stops driving me – it's becoming hell. I'm exhausted.*

I feel like I'm losing touch with reality. I'm dying, suffocating in a deadly atmosphere".

Returning to the central seat of the Aware Ego, facing her business partner, she declares: *"This important part of me is having a very hard time with the hellish pace of our life".*

Raymond, for his part, can better understand the importance of listening to his emotional and physical promptings. In typological terms, this is his Shadow (Introverted Sensing/Extraverted Feeling – Chapter 1, Tables 1.4 and 1.9) speaking:

Raymond – *"I'm really interested in relationships with others, especially children. I am sensitive, and I like to live in the now and not always have to think and plan things."*

After a few months of guidance, their awareness of their different operating styles becomes much more acute.

Crystal – *"One part of me takes up too much space and wants to move too quickly. My extraverted side has become so overdeveloped through my projects, new things, new initiatives. My growth has been in a world where Extraverted Thinking was extremely highly regarded. That's what I developed, from early on, in spite of myself."*

Raymond – *"I find that we have a fantastic project, and nothing is impossible! The challenges that we set together satisfy an important part of me. In every session, I'm curious and above all happy to discover your path and compare our different perspectives – it clarifies a lot of things for me."*

Results

The sharing of roles that occurred at the start-up of the joint business happened naturally, according to both of them. Crystal and Raymond realize at the end of six sessions how much their respective roles were determined by a number of factors related to their social conditioning and by their respective Auto-Pilots.

Crystal – *"I never would have thought that my parents' example would be so meaningful in the way we divided up the responsibilities, or that I was so identified with my Auto-Pilot. My father taught me very early to manage on my own, to grit my teeth and just bear it."*

Raymond – *"I'm very efficient at the things I know how to do, but that's not what I find the most enjoyable now that I'm 50...."*

After ten sessions, the business partners begin to co-create a new division of responsibilities, with a better appreciation of who they are, and where they want to grow.

Crystal – *"What if we shared more of the interactions with the children, so I could start up an online central purchasing agency for Montessori and manage media relationships for the other teaching centers? That would fulfil my needs. I like negotiating for teaching resources and the creativity of a web site. Sometimes I need a bit more quiet activity."*

Raymond – *"With the central purchasing agency, we could fully develop a management consulting program integrating the principles of our school. I would need to know more to strike out in that direction and be innovative: why don't you pass me more of the duties related to teaching and client relationships with the parents and children?"*

Crystal – *"I will continue to oversee the quality and consistency of our teaching program."*

Raymond – *"I can continue taking care of our financial management and written communications with the government departments."*

Crystal – *"I think our couple relationship is stronger, and our business partnership is calmer and more durable. We are better prepared and more fulfilled, and that is holding up over time: even for an "old" couple, it's no small feat to achieve the miracle five-year mark in a shared business!"*

COACHING BUSINESS ASSOCIATES

Delphine Tariot

Intelligence of Self appears to be an approach which is perfectly well adapted to the coaching of business associates, as it contributes to the development of constructive, durable relationships. Here is the example of Company X, a drug testing laboratory.

It is managed by two business associates:

> Bernard, type NiTe – INTJ (see Tables 1.3 and 1.6, in Chapter 1),
> and Oscar, type TeNi – ENTJ (Tables 1.6 and 1.3).

Becoming Who You Are with the Intelligence of Self

Bernard and Oscar thus have very similar functions with a different order. They became friends following the creation of the business, and they are aware that it will be important to protect both the friendship and the performance of their joint leadership, so they wish to take stock of their relationship.

To do this, we undertake a review over three sessions, basing the work on the Bonding Patterns described in Chapter 4.

Sessions 1 and 2: Individual Sessions with Each Associate

We start with individual sessions of two hours' duration with each associate. Both sessions are surprising in the depth and sincerity of the contributions. Both associates have a deep appreciation for the other, both complement the other, and at the time of the coaching work, they are both at a stage we call a "positive" Bonding Pattern – this is a win-win situation for both, and both are happy. The strengths in each of them compensate for the vulnerabilities in the other.

Here is the positive Bonding Pattern described by Bernard:

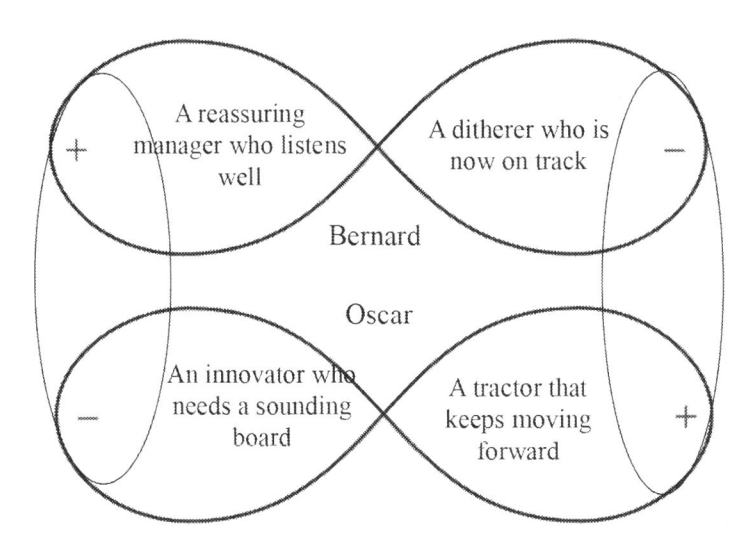

Figure 9.1 Positive Bonding Pattern described by Bernard

And as it is described by Oscar:

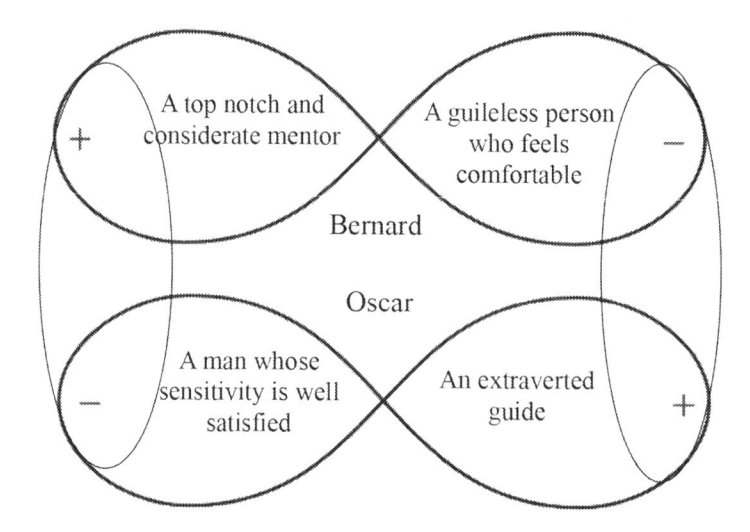

```
           A top notch and        A guileless person
       +   considerate mentor     who feels          −
                                  comfortable

                        Bernard

                         Oscar

           A man whose
       −   sensitivity is well    An extraverted
           satisfied              guide              +
```

Figure 9.2 Positive Bonding Pattern described by Oscar

The two scenarios, which generally look quite similar, clearly illustrate the very enjoyable complementarity that is experienced by both partners. However, in their case, it is important to imagine the "negative" Bonding Pattern to safeguard against it. In fact, by determining what could potentially disrupt their relationship pattern, currently working so well, they will learn to be proactive in recognizing the signs of communication and interpersonal difficulties, which could harm the relationship: "Forewarned is forearmed".

During coaching, this is a complicated exercise. Although a negative Bonding Pattern can arise very quickly in a situation of interpersonal conflict, it can be much more difficult to imagine this occurring from the current reality of a very positive situation, such as Bernard and Oscar's positive Bonding Pattern.

After much discussion and thought, we manage to come up with a somewhat "forced" negative Bonding Pattern, which is possible if not probable.

Becoming Who You Are with the Intelligence of Self

Here is the negative Bonding Pattern as it is imagined by Bernard:

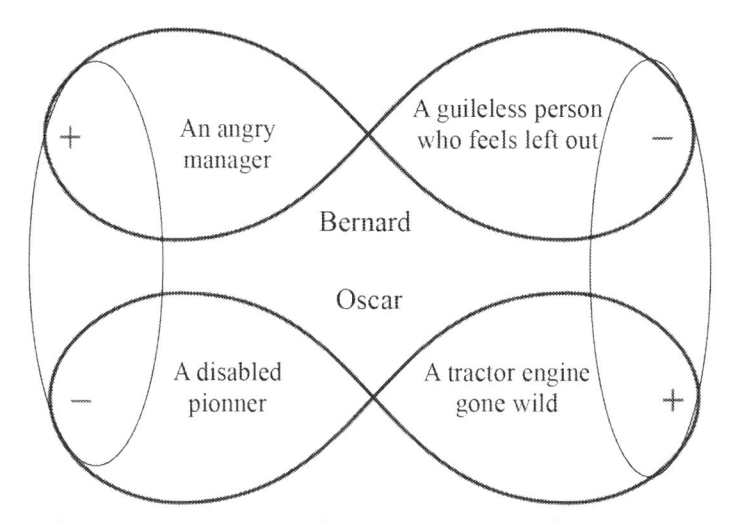

Figure 9.3 Negative Bonding Pattern imagined by Bernard

And as it is imagined by Oscar:

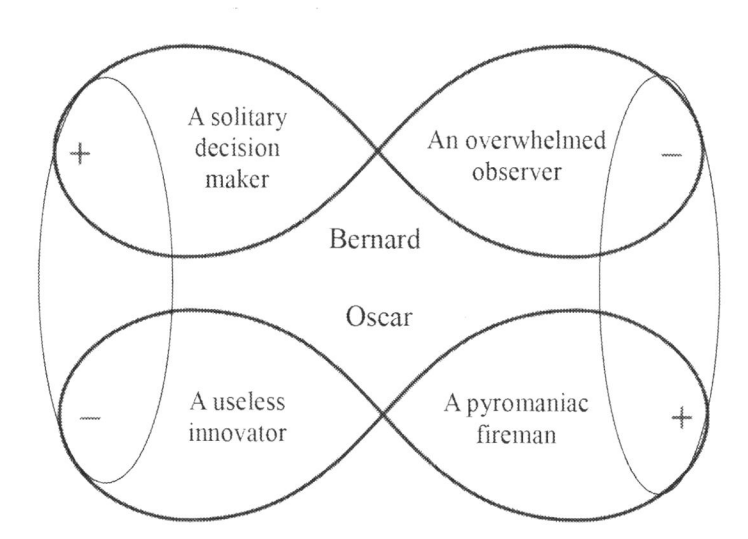

Figure 9.4 Negative Bonding Pattern imagined by Oscar

Although these scenarios are seen as very unlikely at this stage of the relationship, both participants leave feeling satisfied at having forced themselves to complete the exercise. In fact, having verbalized their fears, they can remain alert when faced with situations where one might appear threatening to the other.

At the end of the individual sessions, we reflect on:

- The risks of a positive Bonding Pattern, notably the temptation to rely too heavily on the associate for things that would require more effort and the mobilization of a hidden or disowned Sub-Personality.
- The axes of development (development directions) for each individual. The objective is for each of them to develop within themselves the same strength identified in the associate in order to extend their own individual autonomy. Each develops himself in order to depend less on the other.

Session 3: Sharing the Bonding Patterns – Both Associates Present

We begin with each associate presenting his vision of the positive Bonding Pattern playing out between them, as it was described in the individual session. As the positive scenarios are very similar, we can easily arrive at a scenario which is shared by both associates.

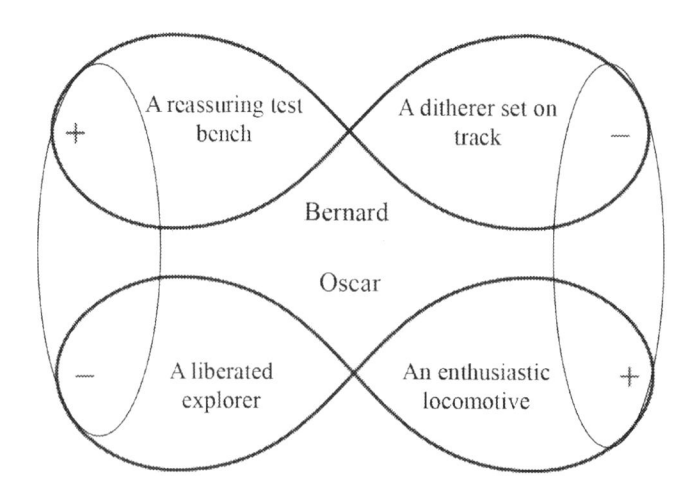

Figure 9.5 Shared Vision of Positive Bonding Pattern

Becoming Who You Are with the Intelligence of Self

We consider this again, but this time, we all focus on the risks that can result from the positive Bonding Pattern. They each recognize the risk of overspecialization, and from that, the need for each associate to acquire some of the capabilities of the other.

For example: Bernard would gain from developing his ability to be more involved in the action, rather than leaning on Oscar to speed things up and get things happening. As for Oscar, he could develop his listening and people skills. This would relieve some of the pressure on Bernard, who would then not have to constantly "lend a friendly ear", which he quite enjoys, but which could be exhausting for him in the long run.

Then we move on to the negative scenario.

We reverse the order of the associates' presentations to balance out the speaking time and facilitate the participation of the introverted associate. Each one describes his negative Bonding Pattern and, according to him, the principal causes behind it. The other reformulates and reacts. As the negative scenarios were imagined by each of them quite differently, this stage of sharing takes more time. At the end, we have three hypothetical negative Bonding Patterns. The two associates retain the hypothesis presented below, although they consider it very unlikely.

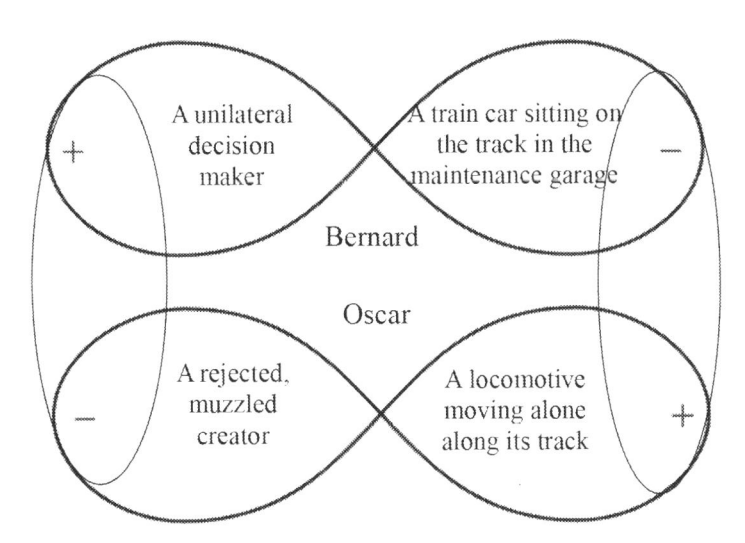

Figure 9.6 Shared Vision of Negative Bonding Pattern

Oscar and Bernard – "We share a common foundation which will prevent us from sliding off course. When we get worked up, we straighten things out, we leave our emotions out of it, and we come up with the same answers."

We end with a few minutes of individual reflection in order to conclude with the lessons learned in the session. The associates understand the necessity of envisioning a negative Bonding Pattern in order to remain on guard against it.

One important point: they both come out of the experience feeling reassured by the interpretations that they might tend to make regarding the actions of the other. Additionally, at this point, they share stories about issues that caused problems in the past, and we notice and compare the different perceptions in these instances of communication.

> For example: Oscar declares that he had difficulty with not always being consulted by Bernard for certain decisions. At those times, Oscar imagined that his opinion was not important to Bernard.
>
> Bernard expresses that it was just negligence and that he was trying to save time and decide quickly, and he did it without realizing the result it would have on Oscar.

Having completed the work, we decide to reconvene on an annual basis, following the same method. This will permit us to evaluate their development and preserve this special time for exchanges and reflections on their relationship.

Beyond this example, I have interviewed a number of business associates in order to get a clear picture of their goals and their reservations about this process of being accompanied by a coach. It requires the participants to be humble, to be willing to question themselves, to be open in front of others, to accept criticism, and to grow.

Some associates, due to their personal background and personality, may be at different stages of development, and thus not be ready to begin coaching at the same time. Coaching of only one of the associates can still be considered a good interim solution in the case of resistance or reluctance, and it can still provide benefit for both parties. The associate who first undertakes the coaching can be joined later by one or more individuals who have noticed the positive growth of their colleague.

USING INTELLIGENCE OF SELF
TO HELP STUDENT GROUPS

Raphaël Bary

Of all the qualities of Intelligence of Self, the one I appreciate the most is its flexibility and the way it can be adapted to a wide range of problems and situations; I undoubtedly feel this way because my facilitation practice takes place in a rather atypical environment. As an instructor and researcher in an engineering school, I do both individual and group coaching, since our students, in groups of four or five, are required to design an industrial project over a period of eight months in order to develop their management skills and to apply engineering methods studied in their various courses in innovation.

During a group facilitation, it occurred to me that Intelligence of Self is as relevant at the collective level as it is at the individual level.

That particular morning, four students wished to talk to me about their project, initiated some seven weeks earlier, and about the difficulties they were having establishing a relationship with the faculty member who was supervising their work. They felt that they were faced with a paradoxical directive: on the one hand, their supervisor was asking them to work autonomously, to be creative, and to come up with a maximum number of new ideas in order to establish the direction of their project, but at the same time, they definitely felt that the supervisor had already formed a precise idea as to the direction their project should take, without, however, telling them explicitly. Should they insist and push their ideas forward and put their own stamp on the project, or alternatively, work to fulfil their supervisor's aspirations? In other words, should they "please themselves" or "please the other" – their supervisor?

As a facilitator's role is not to provide external solutions, but rather to help the participants find their own path to a resolution, each member in turn was given the opportunity to verbalize the way he saw the situation, and what he wished to do. This allowed a shared experience, substantiated by the facts, to be formulated as a way to analyze the situation. At the same time, two opposing visions of what should be done with respect to the supervisor became clear. What predominated was "please the other", their supervisor; this position was defended by three students, who shared Extraverted Feeling (Fe) as a dominant function. This dominance can be seen in the consideration given to meeting the other's needs before the students' own needs. The minority position ("please oneself") was held by the student who had Introverted Thinking (Ti) as a dominant function, and who wished to work first on the ideas generated within the group.

Prior to this point, in working with groups, I had only used the typological approach, retaining Intelligence of Self for individual facilitations. At the group level, psychological type is extremely relevant in team-building and helping clarify relationships, as it offers a common vocabulary that facilitates dialogue, and it posits differences as a source of complementarity, rather than as antagonistic forces. It offers a pertinent diagnostic tool, opening onto possible solutions; however, it is limited. In fact, the typology remains very general and does not describe how the functions are embodied specifically in any one individual. It lacks substance, real life experience, and depth. This was exactly the limit I had reached with this group, and more specifically, with the three students with dominant Extraverted Feeling (Fe). Above all, what drove me to use Intelligence of Self in this case was the tension between the two opposite visions – one dominant and the other disowned – a tension that was at work both within the group and within each student.

After the students had completed the discovery of their psychological type with the CCTI, they were able to explore the Parts through Voice Dialogue, and the work took on a new dimension: each voice was able to express itself more authentically, without interference from its opposite part. In practical terms, I asked the student holding the minority view ("please oneself") to slide his chair away from the others so there would be a spatial separation.

I thus had facing me, physically separated, the two voices of the group. I began by asking the voice wanting to "please the other" to speak up. My original idea was to consider these three students as a whole, but as that didn't work well, I chose one of the students – the most talkative and assertive – to represent the three Extraverted Feeling (Fe). What followed, from that point on, was a relatively typical Voice Dialogue session, except for the fact that, on the one hand, each Sub-Personality was represented by a different person and, on the other hand, no one changed seats during the Voice Dialogue session or during the awareness phase of the session (mainly due to the small size of the room).

Ultimately, it appeared that the initial view "please the other" was based on a vision of teamwork and its underlying values: working together for these students presupposed a gift and counter-gift, and the creation of a community of thought which was essential to the well-being of each member of the team. To the same extent, behind the view "please oneself" was the deep-seated need to finally be able to test oneself and one's worth: the project was seen as an initiation rite in which it was necessary to prove one's ability to become an engineer. The fundamental, archetypal issues underlying the tension appear here: commune with the supervisor or achieve one's initiation. For the students, the session was an opportunity to become aware of what was at stake in the difficulty relating to their supervisor. This also opened up new options by reframing what had been a disjunctive choice *(it must be the supervisor's ideas or our ideas)* into an integrative solution *(how can we succeed in our initiation while also feeling connected to our supervisor?)*. At the end of the day, the students did not identify any immediate, practical solutions, but they decided to clarify the situation with the supervisor, based on their new and deeper understanding of the situation.

Beyond this example, other tools of Intelligence of Self can be used in accompanying student groups, especially Bonding Patterns and projections. They are particularly relevant in helping clarify relationships when tensions arise within a group or between key members working on a project. With projections, it is even possible to have team members work on their positive (or negative) projections in order to improve team cohesiveness.

Based on my experiences, I have found that Intelligence of Self is well adapted to a student population, because these are young people, aware that they are in training, and they are looking for support to help them with the difficulties of group work, because the public school system, with its strong individualistic emphasis, has not prepared them for it. Therefore, they participate relatively willingly in this type of process, even if, as engineering students, they must at first overcome an initial reluctance caused by their intensely Cartesian outlook and analytical minds.

From my perspective as a management instructor, there is a very strong educational impact when a student encounters this type of method in the framework of his training. First of all, it helps students understand more clearly what is playing out within them, and in their relationships; it also helps them see that it is possible to analyze interactions with a very high degree of accuracy, far from their initial impressions marred by prejudice or bias. As well, Intelligence of Self holds the key to developing resolution mechanisms for managerial problems, and these solutions are not limited to sterile alternatives. For example, to resolve conflict, students tend either to keep quiet in order to respect a superficial appearance of harmony and avoid open conflict, or they move into confrontation mode to "clear the air", "let off steam" or "tell it like they see it". And these two ways of

acting, in the short and medium term, create more conflict than they resolve. Finally, this approach is consistent with our humanistic vision of a management function in which performance is not achieved at the cost of the well-being of the members of the collective work enterprise, but rather, thanks to it.

INTELLIGENCE OF SELF AND PROJECTIONS

Carole Dehais

In Chapter 4 we looked at the importance of projections – they can not only disrupt our relationships with others, but, if we are able to overcome them, they also offer us a very important development path. In fact, they probably represent one of the best means of attaining awareness of Self and detachment from the Operating Ego.

J'aime ona Pangaïa, a very experienced Voice Dialogue facilitator, has developed an exercise which allows each individual to become aware of the process of projection. The exercise is based on four questions[30]:

1. What is the fault/attitude that I can't stand in the other? (column 3 in Table 9.1 below: *How I see the other*).
2. What is the opposite of this attitude, the way I see myself? (column 2: *How I see myself*).

---

[30] J'aime ona Pangaïa, *An Introduction to Voice Dialogue – Finding the Benefit of People Who Bug You*

3. What is the advantage that is hidden in this fault/attitude that I can't stand in the other? What would the other say about himself? (column 4: *How the other sees himself*).
4. What is the fault hidden in my attitude? What would the other say of me? (column 1: *How the other sees me*).

This approach has been used effectively:

- In coaching of individuals; and
- In team-building work.

Coaching Individuals

During coaching sessions, it is fairly common for an individual to talk about relationship difficulties encountered with a business associate, a co-worker or the management chain. This can bring things to a standstill. It can therefore be interesting to have the client express the reasons for his annoyance; he makes a list of adjectives describing everything that he can't stand about the other. There is at once a sense of freedom which allows him to become aware of his own "flaws" or "extremes".

It is not particularly difficult to work through questions 1 and 2 in a very thorough fashion, but things get more complicated with questions 3 and 4. Finding a positive quality in the faults of the other can at times seem impossible: the Auto-Pilot feels like it is denying its own values and going astray trying to find the positive where, in its eyes, there is only negative. As for question 4, here again, the Auto-Pilot feels "insulted" and cannot admit to a negative interpretation of the qualities it values.

It is our detachment, creating distance from the Auto-Pilot, which allows the Aware Ego to emerge and thus "lift" or take back the initial projection. This exercise enables the client to become aware of the process. Once that projection has been taken back, the individual can then begin to reintegrate, in part, the quality that was missing in him – in other words, move on to integrating this shadow part that is also a part of the person.

Pierre Cauvin – Geneviève Cailloux

Team Building or Team Coaching

This exercise can be very powerful when done in a group, but there are several precautions that must be taken prior to using it. The most important of these is to ensure that absolute trust and freedom of expression exist between the boss and the team, and between the members of the team. To do this, it is often necessary, between the initial framing of the request by the management chain and HR and the workshop itself, to conduct individual interviews. Respect for these precautions will allow all participants to engage fully in the process.

Another safety precaution, necessary to avoid any blunders or difficulties that might arise, is spending time at the start of the workshop explaining the rules of the process (autonomy, goodwill, confidentiality).

In order for this exercise to have the full impact, the participants must know their type, which will enable them to fully understand the judgments they may feel toward the others. This is equally true for individual work.

Knowing one's type also highlights the cross-projections that exist between individuals who have a preference for different polarities. When there is an atmosphere of goodwill, this can be an entertaining and profound way to go beyond one's judgments about the Other and to accept him – no longer in spite of the differences, but in recognition of the complementarity that can been seen. Understanding the other's mode of operation is often a way to start untangling difficult situations or conflicts within a team. It is also a way to rehabilitate the one or the few individuals who function very differently from the general operating style of the rest of the group.

The answers given are very typical of the type, both in terms of what is valued and in terms of what is judged negatively –specifically this is most often the opposite operating style. Regardless of the benefits felt by the participants, it is therefore possible to tabulate the results in order to create an overview of "typical" projections. As an example, here is a chart summarizing answers to the four questions listed above. These answers were given by participants with an ISTJ profile over the course of a variety of workshops and coaching sessions.

Table 9.1 – Answers Given by ISTJ Participants

(4) How the other sees me	(2) How I see myself	(1) How I see the other	(3) How the other sees himself
Critical	Factual: the facts don't lie	Bad faith; a manipulator	Clever; able to juggle things
Demanding Irritating	Trustworthy	The ones you can't trust	I do my best
Inflexible Rigid	Practical	Always "Me", "I"	Able to tackle all topics
An idiot Gets walked on	Humble	Arrogant	Know how to be assertive
Gets cheated/ taken advantage of	Generous	Opportunist	I make the most of opportunities
Boring	Humble	Braggart/boastful Overly proud	Interesting
Invasive	Like to take on projects	Weak	Take the time
Doesn't stand out Lacks confidence	Uncomplicated	Pretentious Self-important Full of himself	Proud of what I am
Perfectionist	Right to the end Get it done	Negligent	Multi-tasker
Predictable	Loyal	Temperamental	Able to put myself out front
Too nice for his own good	Intellectually honest	Dishonest	Know how to steer
Impersonal/Never reveals himself	Good listener	Selfish	Able to listen to myself
Dangerous	Direct Frank	Two-faced	I take control
Withdrawn	Reserved/Quiet	Blabbermouth	Get recognized

Gets walked on A follower Takes second place	Fair Just	Never admits his errors	I know how to promote myself
Wishy-washy Spineless	Humble	Hustler Social climber	I know how to gain recognition for my true worth
Inconspicuous	Objective Fair	Pretentious	Sure of myself Confident
Insensitive	Steady temper	Moody	Transparent in everything I am and say
Too direct Intolerant	Determined	Indecisive	I think deeply
Stifling	Constantly learning	Mr. Know-it-All	Convinced

Without going too deeply into analyzing these answers, we can easily see the main typological characteristics targeted in each column:

- Columns 3 and 4: Extraverted Intuiting (Ne) or the combination of Extraversion and Perceiving (EP) – the ability to improvise and adapt can be seen negatively (column 3) or positively (column 4);
- Columns 2 and 1: Introverted Sensing (Si) or the combination of Introversion and Judging (IJ) – the discipline, thoroughness, and rigor can be seen positively (column 2) or negatively (column 1).

A Research Project

To date, we have collected the responses of 171 participants. The representation of all types within this sample is currently quite unequal; it depends greatly on the sector of activity and on the position. For this reason, we continue collecting data in order to obtain a sufficient number of responses for each type. It will then be possible to move on to statistical analyses which may allow us to validate – or not – the following hypotheses:

- The positive qualities which individuals of the same type attribute to themselves are shared, and these are different from the qualities that the other types attribute to themselves; and
- The negative characteristics attributed to the others are most commonly the negated counterpart of the opposite type.

The confirmation of these hypotheses will give an original validation of the notion of psychological type.

Conclusion

CONCILING OPPOSITES TO DISCOVER THE INTEGRATED SELF

THE PATH TOWARD INDIVIDUATION, the path of our self-development, resembles a mountain hike: scarcely have we reached one summit when another can be seen off in the distance. For that reason, there can be no question here of a final, definitive conclusion; we offer more of a rest stop along the path. For all that, there is no cause to lose hope: "The struggle itself toward the heights is enough to fill a man's heart. One must imagine Sisyphus happy".[31]

At each stage, in fact, new horizons stretch before our eyes. Our steps become more certain, we don't fall as often, we are quicker to get back on our feet. Unknown vistas beckon. Rather than limping along on one leg, we progress using both. To reach this level, we must do deep work: this is revealed in the dream recounted by Luke, a former elite athlete who has just found out that he has a serious medical problem.

> I dream that I'm organizing a marathon. The runners are in the starting blocks, but I can't let them start because there is some underground work that needs to be done, otherwise the stadium will collapse. The Works Department won't authorize me to do it – they are taking their time.

Luke's Auto-Pilot likes to move quickly; it would like the race to start as quickly as possible. But his Aware Ego, the "Works Department" knows that work at depth, underground, is necessary for the race to be run under optimal conditions. Some of the distance has already been covered, for in his dream, Luke's various parts are already differentiated. The Aware Ego exists and doesn't want to let the primary Sub-Personalities race off at their usual high speed. It wants the Shadow side to be recognized, accepted, integrated. And this requires a different rhythm.

---

[31] Albert Camus, *Le mythe de Sisyphe*, Gallimard, 1985.

How can this integration occur? We can observe it in Zoe's dream.

We met Zoe earlier (Chapter 2) – her Auto-Pilot always pushed her to make sacrifices for others. Since then, she has worked hard on conciling the two opposites, namely:

- her Auto-Pilot, who drives her to exhaustion in the name of always doing more for others (Extraverted Feeling as dominant). She has, furthermore, just undergone back surgery for a herniated disc.
- her inferior function, Introverted Thinking, which at the beginning seemed cold and distant to her, but which gradually enables her to step back so she can establish priorities and protect herself.

At the end of her training, Zoe shares the following dream, where we can see at first opposition followed by integration between Feeling (F) and Thinking (T):

> I had a very "strange and penetrating"[32] dream where the **f**jord of the **F**s came in contact with the **t**errain of the **T**s. In this dream, there were two worlds, separated by two walls.
>
> On the left, it looked like a **T**etris game, all black and white, with "**T**"s falling and locking into others. It was a cold and remote world, like **T**hinking.
>
> On the right, there was a beautiful **f**ield of **f**abulously colored **f**lowers, it upli**f**ted my heart just looking at it. It was the world of the "**F**"s, e**ff**usive and full of emotive **f**eeling.
>
> All at once, there was a **t**errible **st**orm. The **t**hunder roared and the lightning struck. And then, I saw the **H** of a hospital. In this hospital, there were two types of service – psychiatry, for the **f**reaks and orthopedics for the **T**hinkers.
>
> In the psychiatric service for the **f**reaks, the caregivers are **F**s who play paintball against the **T**s. To avoid being hit by the paint bullets, the **T**s throw themselves at the wall, which **f**inally **t**umbles down.

---

[32] Paul Verlaine – Mon rêve familier

In the orthopedic service, the caregivers are **T**s who torture the
Fs. They want to rip off that little bar and put it on the other side
of their heads and transform them into **T**s. The **F**s cry, and cry...
for so long that their **t**ears make the wall mel**t**.

And once the two walls are gone, the two worlds unite to create
one world:

The **F**s "mor**f**" into **f**lowers.

The **T**s **t**ip upside down on**t**o their **t**ops and **t**urn into strong
stems.

And every stem **f**inally **f**inds its **f**lower....

Thus, moving beyond confrontation and antagonism, a larger world opens up before us, the world of conciled opposites. We are called to let go of our illusions, renounce our judgments and our need to be right. At each stage, we are required to take back our projections and reappropriate what we are unwilling or unable to acknowledge within ourselves.

But over time each one of us may find wholeness and become an autonomous being, undivided and indivisible. And then each one of us may also accept and understand the Other for what it is, and not for what we want it to be. And so, our own self-development becomes a contribution to the development of the human community as a whole.

Glossary

Adaptation strategies: An overall group of attitudes and behaviors adopted by an individual to respond to demands from the external environment.

Anima: The unconscious female component of the male personality. It may assume a positive or negative aspect. Its presence is manifested in relations with women.

Animus: The unconscious male component of the female personality. It may assume a positive or negative aspect. Its presence is manifested in relations with men.

Attitudes: In the broadest sense, an attitude is a predisposition of the psyche to act or react in a specific direction. The two poles of the psyche's dimension that provide its orientation toward the outer or exterior world (extraversion) or toward the inner or interior world (introversion) are more specifically designated by the term "attitudes". By extension, the J/P index is also classified as an attitude.

Auto-Pilot: Combination of processes and strategies that spontaneously take control of an individual (equivalent to the Operating Ego and the Primary Self).

Aware Ego: Ongoing or continual process of integrating opposite polarities.

Bonding Pattern: System of interactions between the various Sub-Personalities of both individuals involved in a relationship.

CCTI (Cailloux-Cauvin Type Indicator): Typological indicator, developed by Geneviève Cailloux and Pierre Cauvin, which facilitates the discovery of one's own type.

Cognitive Processes: Operating system of the psyche; a variety of processes by which we achieve awareness.

Differentiation: Process which enables functions to separate from one another in order to be able to play their specific role without contamination. Undifferentiated functions are archaic, unconscious, and manifested in an ambivalent way.

Disidentification (Disidentify): The process by which a person becomes aware that a part of him tends to take up too much space or even consider that it is, itself, the entire person. Similar terms that we have used to refer to this process are: "disidentify", "detach", "separate", and "unhook". "Unhook" is a term used by Hal and Sidra Stone in their work.

Disowned (Self/Selves): Term used to designate of a Self that is not recognized, either because it has not previously manifested, or because it has been rejected.

Ego: For Jung, the center of consciousness.

Entropy: Term relating to thermodynamics, indicating the progressive degradation of a system towards a state of increasing disorder.

Extraversion: Term utilized by Jung to indicate the orientation of an individual's energy toward the external world.

Feeling: One of two judging functions, based on personal and subjective values.

Function dynamics: Role that the functions play within each type. All the functions have a clearly differentiated place and role within the psyche, and this creates specific dynamics. In this way, we can distinguish dominant, auxiliary, tertiary, and inferior functions.

Functions: For Jung, there are four psychic processes of perceiving (Sensing and Intuiting) and judging or evaluating (Thinking and Feeling). These functions are operating styles, and as such, must be distinguished from the content(s) of the psyche, which are sensations, intuitions, thoughts, and feelings. Functions are always written in the singular form, with a capital letter.

Auxiliary function: This is the second function in psychic development. It balances the dominant in terms of the nature of the function and the orientation of the energy.

Dominant function: This is the primary function in psychic development. It establishes the general nature of the psyche.

Inferior function: This is the function opposite the dominant. It is the most closely connected to the unconscious.

Tertiary function: This is the function opposite the auxiliary. It introduces the inferior function or blocks access to it.

Function-Attitude: The eight judging and perceiving functions with their orientation toward the inner or outer world, namely: Extraverted Sensing (Se), Introverted Sensing (Si), Extraverted Intuiting (Ne), Introverted Intuiting (Ni), Extraverted Thinking (Te), Introverted Thinking (Ti), Extraverted Feeling (Fe), Introverted Feeling (Fi)

Individuation: Process by which a person becomes a psychological individual, in other words, an autonomous and indivisible unit, a whole.

Introversion: Term used by Jung to indicate the orientation of an individual's energy toward the inner world.

Intuition or Intuiting: One of the two perceiving functions; it is characterized by a global nature, immediate and focused on the field of potentialities.

Judging: The word has three different meanings. It can:

- Refer to the judging or decision-making functions (Thinking, Feeling).
- Designate one of the two poles of the "Lifestyle" dimension.
- Indicate the disapproval expressed by one Sub-Personality in relation to another.

Negentropy: Opposite of entropy, leading thus to an increase in the energy potential of a system. An inflow of information is one of the principle factors of negentropy.

Operating Ego: Equivalent to the Auto-Pilot.

Part: See Self

Perception or Perceiving: The word has two different meanings. It can:

- Refer to the perceiving functions (Sensing, Intuiting).
- Designate one of the two poles of the "Lifestyle" dimension.

Projection: Process by which we attribute to another person or external object one of our own characteristics. The process of projection occurs unconsciously. The work of individuation most notably consists in gradually detaching from our projections to establish a true relationship with the reality of the other person or object.

Primary Ego or Primary Self: Equivalent to the Operating Ego or the Auto-Pilot.

Psyche: The entire group of psychic phenomena considered as forming a person's individuality. This includes the contents of psychic life – notably feelings, thoughts, and emotions – as well as the processes or operating styles (for example, decision-making, projection mechanisms, and many others).

Sensation or Sensing: One of the two perceiving functions; it is characterized by attention to the facts, the sense of reality.

Self/Selves: For Jung, the center between the conscious (Self) and the unconscious. Only used in the singular. In Voice Dialogue, it is also used to designate a part of the individual, and in this context, it is also used in the plural (Selves). The Selves or Sub-Personalities represent the crystallization of the strategies and processes, which Jung also called "complexes". In Voice Dialogue, "voice" and "part" are synonymous with a Self.

Sub-Personality: See Self

Shadow: The opposite of consciousness with which it has a dynamic relationship.

Thinking: One of the judging functions, based on rational and objective logic.

Voice: See Self

Voice Dialogue: Voice Dialogue, known as "Dialogue intérieur" in France, was developed by Hal and Sidra Stone starting in 1970. The term includes an aspect of general theory, which was the main inspiration for the first part of this book, as well as a methodological component, which is described in Chapter 7.

Index Of Literary References

The individuals indicated by the symbol † in the text and listed in this section are chosen to illustrate a particular personality type or typological function which can be seen in some of their described characteristics. This does not allow us to deduce their "real" type, which, by definition, can only be discovered by the individual, from within.

Abbé (Abbot) Pierre (Fi) – French priest who helped the homeless, creating an organization to support them (Emmaüs). Considered for many years the most popular person in France, he remained faithful to his personal principles, which were often in contradiction to civil institutions and the Catholic church.

Alexander the Great (Te) – King of Macedonia in the 4th century BC. Conquered an immense empire extending from Egypt to northwestern India. Military and administrative brilliance.

Ant and the Grasshopper (Si/Se) – One of the most famous fables of Jean de la Fontaine (1621-1695), contrasting the frugal and forward-looking ant with the profligate and devil-may-care grasshopper.

Apollo (Ni) – God of music, song, and divination. Symbolizes reason, clarity, order.

Augustine (St) – Father of the Church in the 4th century AD and author, most notably, of "Confessions", "On the Trinity", and "The City of God". The quotation, expressing a perpetual need to push beyond one's limits, is attributed to him.

Boileau – Nicolas Boileau (1636-1711), author of "Art poétique". Some of the lines of "Art poétique", such as the one quoted, have become commonplace sayings.

Camus – Albert Camus (1913-1960), French writer, winner of the Nobel Prize for Literature. In his work "The Myth of Sisyphus", Camus repeats Shuzo Kuki's phrase "…we must imagine Sisyphus happy…", signifying that man finds happiness in the completion of a set task, and not in the content of the task itself.

Clarke/Kubrick – "A Space Odyssey", a novel by Arthur C. Clarke and a film by Stanley Kubrick. During a space voyage, Hal, the onboard computer, tries to overcome the astronauts on board and take control of the spaceship.

Cyrano de Bergerac (Fi) – Main character of Edmond Rostand's eponymous play (1896). Cyrano is a romantic hero whose unattractive physique shelters a heart brimming with love that he only reveals to Roxane at the very end of his life.

Davis, Angela (Fe) – Political activist, scholar, and author (1944-). Defender of social values, she emerged as a prominent counterculture radical in the 1960s (a leader of the Communist Party, USA, involved in Civil Rights movement, etc.).

Demeter (Fe) – Goddess of the earth and harvests and archetype of the mother rushing to the aid of her daughter Persephone, who was carried off by Hades. (Roman equivalent of Demeter is Ceres)

Diderot (Si) – Denis Diderot (1713-1784), Age of Enlightenment philosopher, disinclined to public controversy. Editor of the famous "Encyclopédie".

Dionysus (Se) – Dionysus is the god of dance and frenzied, spontaneous music. Lives freely, even giving himself over to excess, as he is also the god of wine (Roman equivalent, Bacchus).

Einstein (Ti) – Albert Einstein (1879-1955), one of the greatest minds of all time, winner of the Nobel Prize in physics, author of the theory of relativity. His formula "E=MC²" is a perfect example of the search for a concise, underlying explanation that is typical of Introverted Thinking.

Epimenides – Greek poet/philosopher (8th century BC). The paradox of the Cretan is attributed to him: "All Cretans are liars, says the Cretan." This paradox contradicts the principle of the excluded third and has for centuries generated collective debate among logicians.

Freud, Sigmund – Austrian neurologist known as the "father of pychoanalysis" (1856-1939). "Dreams are the royal road to the unconscious", from "Five Lectures on Psychoanalysis", 1910.

Gandhi (Ni) – Mahatma Gandhi (1869-1948), India's spiritual guide, leader of the independence movement based on nonviolence. His vision has inspired many leaders throughout the world.

Gaultier, Jean-Paul (Ne) – Born in 1952 Jean-Paul Gaultier is a French fashion designer known for his originality and his ability to innovate and change.

General de Gaulle (Ni) – Charles de Gaulle (1890-1970), leader of the French Resistance movement and former President of the French Republic. The first sentence of his published memoirs is typical example of Introverted Intuiting: "All my life I have had a certain idea of France."

Girl with a Pearl Earring (Si) – *The Girl with a Pearl Earring* is a painting (circa 1665) by Johannes Vermeer. A novel of the same title was written by Tracy Chevalier, recounting the story of Griet, a servant who poses for Vermeer and describes in detail the life of the Vermeer family.

Giroud, Françoise – French journalist (1916-2003), writer, politician. Deputy Minister of Women's Affairs from 1974-1976.

Grasshopper: See (The) Ant and the Grasshopper.

Hepburn, Audrey (Fi) – Archetype of quiet grace, "ranked" as the third best actress of all time. Dedicated much energy to her tasks as ambassador for UNICEF.

Hephaestus (Si) – God of blacksmiths and fire. Creator of articles, he is the only god on Olympus able to "fabricate". (Roman equivalent, Vulcan).

Hera (Fe) – Sister and wife of Zeus, Hera is the protector of women, guardian of marriage and procreation. Very attached to family values; suffers greatly from the many affairs of her unfaithful husband. (Roman equivalent, Juno).

Hermes (Ne) – Hermes is the messenger of the gods, the god of travelers, business…and thieves! Trickster god, resourceful and cunning, able to deal with unexpected situations. (Roman equivalent, Mercury)

Hestia (Fi) – Hestia is the oldest of the gods, unchanging and virginal. She is the guardian of the home and private hearth, not needing public worship. In Rome, her priestesses were the Vestal Virgins. (Roman equivalent, Vesta)

Hillman, James – James Hillman (1926-2011) was a psychoanalyst and author of numerous works. He was director of the Jung Institute in Zürich and developed archetypal psychoanalysis.

Jung, CG (Ti) – Carl Gustav Jung (1875-1961) was a Swiss psychiatrist/medical doctor who founded analytical psychology. The Intelligence of Self approach is directly inspired by his work. Jung defined his own type as Introverted Thinking dominant with Extraverted Intuiting as auxiliary.

Kant (Ti) – Emmanuel Kant (1724-1804), German philosopher. His profound thinking is typical of Introverted Thinking.

Le Nôtre (Te) – André Le Nôtre (1613-1700) was a landscape architect and principal gardener for Louis XIV. He designed numerous gardens in the orderly, structured "French style".

Leonardo da Vinci (Ni) – One of the greatest, multi-talented geniuses to have lived (1452-1519). His capacity to imagine the future and turn it into reality is typical of Introverted Intuiting.

Lincoln (Fi) – Abraham Lincoln (1809-1865), 16th President of the United States of America. A determined abolitionist, he lay the groundwork to preserve the Union as best he could.

MacGyver (Se) - Angus MacGyver is a TV series special agent whose main characteristics are his practical skills, his trouble-shooting abilities and his unflappable attitude.

Marco Polo (Ne) – Venetian merchant (1254-1324), archetype of the explorer. After a journey of 26 years in the Far East, he wrote his "Book of the Marvels of the World".

Marie-Antoinette (Se) – Marie-Antoinette of Austria (1755-1793), wife of Louis XIV, King of France. Known for her taste for seemingly simple but luxurious and elitist pleasures, she escaped the weighty rules of the royal court to the extent possible. Criticized for her frivolity, she courageously met her end at the guillotine.

Marius and Olive - Two fictitious characters from southern France whose actions and adventures take on an often absurd or exaggerated aspect; they are often recounted as "tall tales" ("galéjade").

Martin Luther King (Ni) – Baptist minister (1929-1968) famous for his nonviolent struggle against racial segregation and for peace. His famous speech "I have a dream…." opened a door to a new future.

Mary Poppins (Fe) – Main character of one of Hollywood's most famous films, extolling love, family life, respect of children and diversity.

Mother Theresa (Fe) – Roman Catholic sister (1910-1997) who spent her life in service to the poor. She founded a religious congregation "Missionaries of Charity".

de Musset, Alfred – French dramatist (1810-1857), poet, and novelist who penned *La Nuit de mai*; the pelican has long been a symbol of a father sacrificing himself to feed his children.

Napoléon (Te) – Napoléon Bonaparte (1769-1821), emperor of France. An unequalled military strategist, he conquered a vast portion of Europe. Thanks to his talent for organization, the administrative structures that he implemented endure in France a full two centuries later.

Nietzsche (Ti) – Friedrich Nietzsche (1844-1900), professor of philology turned philosopher. His work represents a radical criticism of human values.

Pascal – Blaise Pascal (1623-1662) mathematician, physicist, inventor, philosopher, and theologian. Published posthumously, his "Thoughts" are a collection of notes and reflections which provide a wealth of aphorisms and paradoxes; it is one of the most important works of French literature.

Perfume: The Story of a Murderer (Si) – Best-seller written by Patrick Süskind. The book is referenced here to illustrate the depth of perception of Introverted Sensing types.

Perrette (The Milk Maid and Milk Pail) (Ne) – One of the most well-known fables written by Jean de la Fontaine (1621-1695). Recounts the tale of a young farm girl on her way to market. She dreams of how she can make a fortune by "trading up", starting with her pail of milk and making a series of trades. And then she trips and spills the pail of milk that she was intending to sell.

Peter Pan (Ne) – Character created in 1902 by J.M. Barrie. He is the archetype of the eternal child who does not want to grow up, living forever in a fairy world. In this respect, he is a notable illustration of the "puer aeternus" described by Jung.

Plautus – Roman comedic playwright (254-184 BC). The quotation is taken from "Asinaria" *(The One with the Asses)*.

Pope Jean-Paul II (Fe) – Karol Wojtyla (1920-2005) became Pope in 1978. He is included as the model for a new form of evangelism; he traveled the world during his papacy, bringing together enormous crowds.

Prometheus (Ti) – One of the Titans (primordial Greek deities) who, after having created man, earth, and water, gives man fire and mastery of metallurgy. He is sentenced to an eternal punishment by Zeus until Hercules liberates him from his torture. He then becomes immortal.

Racine – Jean Racine (1639-1699) French playwright and poet. The quotation is taken from *Britannicus*, Act II, scene 3.

Robinson Crusoe (Se) – Novel published in 1719 by Daniel Defoe. It describes the very practical way in which the hero manages to survive after being shipwrecked on a deserted island.

Sherlock Homes (Si) – Detective character created in 1887 by Sir Arthur Conan Doyle. One of the detective's main talents is his ability to observe all the details of a given situation.

Shiva – Hindu god taking many forms, one of which is Shiva Narajah, represented as having four arms.

Socrates (Ti) – Famous Greek philosopher (470-399 BC), known, among other reasons, for his method of questioning (the Socratic method) designed to help an individual discover the truth.

Taylor (Te) – Frederick Winslow Taylor (1856-1915) was a highly influential promoter of the Efficiency Movement (improving industrial efficiency) who wrote "The Principles of Scientific Management".

Voltaire (François-Marie Arouet) – French writer and philosopher (1694-1778). He famously lampooned a rival (Marivaux) for excessive frivolity, inventing the term "marivaudage": the art of "weighing flies' eggs on scales made from a spider's web".

Bibliography

This bibliography includes only the English and French works which directly influenced our thinking. It is in no way intended to be an exhaustive reference.

AGNEL, Aimé. *Jung; La Passion de l'Autre.* Toulouse: Les essentiels Milan, 2004.

BENNET, Angelina. *The Shadows of Type.* Lulu, 2010.

BERENS, Linda. *Dynamics of Personality Type.* Telos Publication, 1999.

CASTLEMAN, Tess. *Threads, Knots, Tapestries; How a Tribal Connection is Revealed through Dreams and Synchronicities.* Syren Book Company, 2003.

CAUVIN, Pierre and Geneviève CAILLOUX.

Deviens qui tu es, 4th edition. Barret: Le Souffle d'Or, 2007.

La dynamique des fonctions. Vernou: Osiris Éditions, 2005.

Embrassez vos opposés. Barret: Le Souffle d'Or, 2007.

Les types de personnalité, ESF, 12th edition. Paris: 2014.

Portraits-Type. Vernou: Osiris Éditions, 2008.

La dynamique du Moi Conscient – Guide du praticien. Vernou: Osiris Éditions, 2006.

L'intelligence de Soi et de l'autre, 2nd edition. Paris: Dunod, 2014

CAUVIN, Pierre. *La cohésion des équipes – Pratique du team building,* 8th edition. Paris: ESF, 2014.

CAUVIN, Pierre. *La situation est grave mais pas désespérée.* Radio broadcast on France Inter and CD. Osiris Éditions, August 2003.

CAUVIN, Pierre and BRIDGES William. *Types d'organisation,* 2nd edition. Vernou: Osiris Éditions, 2005.

DYAK, Myriam. *The Voice Dialogue Facilitator's Handbook.* LIFE Energy Press, 1999.

FRANZ (von), Marie-Louise. "The Inferior Function." in *Jung's Typology,* Spring (1971).

HILLMAN, James.

The Soul's Code; In Search of Character and Calling. Random House, 1996.

"The Feeling Function." in *Jung's Typology,* Spring (1971).

HIRSCH, Sandra and Jean KUMMEROW. *Life Types.* Warner Books, 1989.

HUMBERT, Elie. *Jung.* Presses Pocket, 1983.

JUNG, Carl Gustav. (among other works):

Memories, Dreams, Reflections. Vintage Reissue, 1989.

Psychological Types. Collected Works, Vol. 6. Princeton, 2014.

Mysterium coniunctionis. Princeton, 1989.

Man and his Symbols. Dell, 1968.

Introduction to Jungian Psychology: Notes of the Seminar on Analytical Psychology Given in 1925. Princeton University, 2011.

Modern Man in Search of a Soul. Routledge, 2001.

KÜBLER-ROSS, Elisabeth. *On Grief and Grieving: Finding the Meaning of Grief Through the Five Stages of Loss.* Scribner, 2005.

MILLER, Alice *The Body never Lies.* Norton 2006

MONBOURQUETTE, Jean. *Apprivoiser son ombre.* Bayard, 2001.

MYERS, Isabel. *Gifts Differing.* CPP, 1980.

ONA PANGAÏA, J'AIME. *The Benefit of People Who Bug You*, www.voicedialoguework.com

PEARMAN, Roger, Michael LOMBARDO, and Robert EICHINGER. *You – Being more Effective in your Type.* Loming, 2005.

PINKER, Steven. *The Blank Slate.* Viking Penguin, 2002.

QUENK, Naomi. Beside Ourselves. CPP, 1993.

SHAUBHUT, Nancy and Richard THOMPSON. "MBTI Type Tables for Occupations." CPP, 2008.

SPOTO, Angelo. *Jung's Typology in Perspective.* Chiron Publication, 1995.

STEIN, Murray. *Jung's Map of the Soul,* 7th printing. Chicago and Lasalle: Open Court, 2004.

STONE, Hal and Sidra STONE.

> *Embracing Our Selves.* Nataraj, 1989.
>
> *Embracing Each Other.* Nataraj, 1989.
>
> *Partnering – A New Kind of Relationship.* Nataraj, 2000.

Embracing Your Inner Critic. Harper, 1993.

Analysis of Events of Sept 11th. Newsletters, October 15th and November 18th 2001.

STONE, Sidra. *The Shadow King.* Nataraj, 1997.

THOMPSON, Henry. *Jung's Function-Attitudes Explained.* Wormhole Publishing, 1996.

Acknowledgements

We would like to extend warm thanks to Catherine Carston for the work that she has done. Going beyond the task of translation, Catherine provided helpful assistance through her suggestions and comments. The English version of this book is, for that reason, more complete than the French original! Thanks as well to her translation team: Alix Carrel, Rhonda Hercus, and Norma Pelletier.

We also thank Kim Wall for taking the initiative in proposing the translation and for having encouraged and supported us in a number of ways. Thanks as well to Anna Ivara and Dorsey Cartwright for their unwavering support.

The following individuals contributed to the production of Chapter 9 in the French original ***L'Intelligence de Soi…et de l'autre*** (2009):

Raphaël Bary
Héloïse Blain
Carole Dehais
Isabelle Demeure
Hélène Dercourt
Isabelle Saint Macary
Delphine Tariot

Information, Interventions, Training

THE METHODS PRESENTED in this book are used by Osiris Conseil:

- working within businesses, in the form of individual and team coaching, and
- working with individuals wishing this type of accompaniment.

The methods are also the subject of training seminars, particularly for human resource professionals, consultants, HR employees, coaches, therapists, and psychologists.

Osiris Conseil has 30 years' experience in these areas and offers a full range of seminars at all levels. For further information or to register for training, please contact:

Geneviève Cailloux – Pierre Cauvin
Osiris Conseil
33 rue du Montoir
77670 Vernou – La Celle sur Seine
Tel: +33 1 64 23 03 07
Fax: +33 1 64 23 06 10
Email:
pierre@osiris-conseil.com
genevieve@osiris-conseil.com

In North America contact:

Kim Wall
1225 Walter Gage St
Comox, BC
V9M 3X1
Canada
kimwall102@gmail.com
www.consciousawarenesscounselling.ca
(250) 897-9747

Anna Ivara
112 W. 18th St. #6C
New York, NY
10011
USA
avara3@gmail.com
www.annaivara.com
917-856-1198

Dorsey Cartwright
1714-B Barton Hills Dr
Austin, Texas 78704-2765
512.444.7733
Fax: 512.444.7724
mdcartw@aol.com
www.imagoworks.com/pages/meetdorsey.html

Index Of Illustrations

Figure 1.2 – Olivia's Light functions: Fi/Ne (Introverted Feeling/Extraverted Intuiting) 17
Figure 1.3 – Joseph's shadow functions: Fi/Ne (Introverted Feeling/Extraverted Intuiting) 22
Figure 1.4 – Olivia's shadow functions: Te/Si (Extraverted Thinking/Introverted Sensing) 22
Figure 1.5 – "Opposite" functions for type Te/Si (Extraverted Thinking/Introverted Feeling) 25
Figure 1.6 – "Opposite" functions for type Fi/Ne (Introverted Feeling/Extraverted Intuiting) 25
Figure 2.1 – Function Cross Ni/Te (Introverted Intuiting/Extraverted Thinking) 34
Figure 2.2 – Function Cross Ne/Fi (Extraverted Intuiting/Introverted Feeling) 36
Figure 2.3 – Function Cross Fi/Se (Introverted Feeling/Extraverted Sensing) 37
Figure 2.4 – Unintegrated Self, Se/Fi, of Type Ni/Te (Introverted Intuiting/Extraverted Thinking 45
Figure 2.5 – Unintegrated Self Fi/Si of Type Ne/Fi (Extraverted Intuiting/Introverted Feeling) 46
Figure 2.6 – Shadow of the shadow Ne/Ti of Type Ni/Te (Introverted Intuiting/Extraverted Thinking) 47
Figure 3.1 – Conciling Opposites for Type Fe/Si (Extraverted Feeling/Introverted Sensing) 58
Figure 4.1 – Paul and Valerie's Positive Bonding Pattern 62
Figure 4.2 – Paul and Valerie's negative Bonding Pattern 64
Figure 4.3 – Projections Ni/Te-Se/Fi Introverted Intuiting/Extraverted Thinking and Extraverted Sensing/Introverted Feeling 69
Figure 4.4 – Projection Ti/Se-Te/Ni: Introverted Thinking/Extraverted Sensing and Extraverted Thinking/Introverted Intuiting 70

Figure 5.1 – Positive Bonding Pattern of Couple – Louis and Brigitte . 84
Figure 5.2 – Negative Bonding Pattern of Couple – Louis and Brigitte 86
Figure 6.1 – Positive Bonding Pattern Coach – Client 131
Figure 6.2 – Positive Bonding Pattern Coach – Client Based on
    Fee for Service 132
Figure 6.3 – Positive Bonding Pattern Coach – Client Based on
    Gratification of the Coach 133
Figure 6.4 – Negative Bonding Pattern Coach – Client 135
Figure 6.5 – Possible Development of Negative Bonding Pattern
    Coach – Client 136
Figure 8.1 – Your Function Cross Identify Your Primary Strategies 172
Figure 9.1 Positive Bonding Pattern described by Bernard 199
Figure 9.2 Positive Bonding Pattern described by Oscar 200
Figure 9.3 Negative Bonding Pattern imagined by Bernard 201
Figure 9.4 Negative Bonding Pattern imagined by Oscar 201
Figure 9.5 Shared Vision of Positive Bonding Pattern 202
Figure 9.6 Shared Vision of Negative Bonding Pattern 203

Index Of Tables

Table 1.1 – Summary of the 8 Functions 7
Table 1.2 – Extraverted Sensing (Se) 8
Table 1.3 – Introverted Intuiting (Ni) 9
Table 1.4 – Introverted Sensing (Si) 10
Table 1.5 – Extraverted Intuiting (Ne) 11
Table 1.6 – Extraverted Thinking (Te) 12
Table 1.7 – Introverted Feeling (Fi) 13
Table 1.8 – Introverted Thinking (Ti) 14
Table 1.9 – Extraverted Feeling (Fe) 15
Table 1.10 – The 16 Types 21
Table 1.11 – Order of the Functions 26
Table 2.1 – Adaptation Strategies 29
Table 2.2 – Functions and Strategies 35
Table 4.1 – Projections by One Function onto the Opposite Function .74
Table 4.2 – Projections by One Function onto the Same Function in the Opposite Orientation 74
Table 5.1 – Function Reversal at Midlife 93
Table 9.1 – Answers Given by ISTJ Participants 211

Printed in the United States
By Bookmasters